Better Health Through *Taste*

Easy Transformation With Ayurveda

THE COOKBOOK

JOHN BROOME

BETTER HEALTH THROUGH TASTE

Easy Transformation With Ayurveda

The Cookbook

In association with Living Ayurveda Resources Int., Inc.

Copyright © 2022 by John Broome

All rights reserved. No part of this book may be reproduced, in any form or by any electronic or mechanical means, including information storage and retrieval systems, photocopying, or otherwise without prior written permission from the author, except by reviewers, who may quote brief passages in a review or in critical articles.

Printed in United States of America

Dedication

I dedicate this book to Maharishi Mahesh Yogi, who popularized Ayurveda in the West. This inspired me to bring great Ayurvedic recipes to as many people as possible.

Acknowledgements

I was only able to do this with help from many people I can't name them all here but some of the more supportive collaborators are mentioned here:

Paul & Carol Morehead for always being there for me and for trying out my recipes and giving great feedback. Andrew Stenberg for making the connection between tastes and balance. Rod Hindmarsh from How2Franchise, for his commitment to my broader goals for Ayurveda food products. For Jocelyne Comtois who sees every single detail and makes things happen.

Copywriter Anne Melfi for her clear and concise work.

Patricia Saunders for excellent proof reading.

To everyone else for helping with making the recipes, eating the meals, giving feedback and helping create the words on the page.

Foreword

How to Use This Book

I wrote this book so that anyone can quickly grasp and use Ayurveda in the kitchen, a delicious way to well-being. The recipes are designed to provide quick and easy meals to serve the needs and tastes of different people. With a little briefing on how Ayurveda works, you will be able to use these recipes to cook up dishes that are just right for your own constitution (or mind-body type) and also serve your family and friends with the best of health.

Ayurveda identifies six tastes: sweet, sour, salty, bitter, pungent, and astringent. They correspond to the needs of the three mind-body types which Ayurveda identifies, their preferences, and their requirements for well-being. In this book, you will learn a little about the mind-body types, how to easily identify who is which type, and which recipes will best serve them. You will see how different tastes balance different mind-body types. The controlling principles at work in the herbs, spices, and foods are the same controlling principles that constitute the physiology. Everyone has fire, air, water, etc., in varying proportions as does everything in the universe. For practical purposes, Ayurveda organizes these controlling principles into three categories: Vata, Pitta, and Kapha, the three doshas, which make up the different mind-body types. So, Kapha spices and foods serve to balance a Kapha mind-body constitution, and so forth. Once you learn about the basics, you will know how to recognize who needs what: Are you Vata, Pitta, or Kapha, or some combination of the three? Do you need sweet or salty tastes or would pungent or sour suit you better? You will be able to easily produce meals personalized to your needs because the recipes in this book offer different balances of the six tastes to satisfy both the palate and the appetite.

So, we will start with the story of Ayurveda and the three doshas. Next, you can use the questionnaire at the end of the discussion to discover your own unique mind-body type, your needs, your personality characteristics, your likes, and dislikes which, when heeded, will make you most comfortable and happy. Use your results as a guide to choosing suitable recipes among the 64 selections offered in this book. They make use of three different spice mixes to balance each of the mind-body types. You can also use the spice mixes every day on your own recipes—sandwiches, salads, soups, and whatever you like.

Contents

Dedication	iii
Acknowledgements	iv
Foreword	v
Contents	vi
1 - Introduction to Ayurveda	9
2 - Ayurveda and the Three Doshas	11
3 - How to Create Balance Using the Six Tastes	17
4 - My Vata, Pitta, and Kapha Spice Mixes	22
5 - Introduction to the Recipes	25
1 - Breakfast	31
Vata/Pitta - Oatmeal	32
Kapha - Oatmeal	33
Pitta - Stewed Apples	34
Pitta - Stewed Apple with Raisins & Coconut	35
Vata - Almond Spread	36
Pitta - Sunflower Spread	37
Kapha - Honey Spread	38
2 - Soups	39
Vata/Pitta/Kapha - Vegetable Soup for Everyone	40
Vata/Pitta - Black Bean, Asparagus, Avocado, Quinoa & Sweet Potato Soup	42
Vata - Asparagus and Quinoa Soup	43
Vata/Pitta - Carrot & Cilantro Soup	44
Vata/Pitta - Black Bean, Quinoa & Vegetables Soup	45
Vata/Pitta - Vegetable Soup with French Lentils & Quinoa	47
Vata/Pitta - Cauliflower - Kale Soup	49
Kapha - Stew with Black Bean & Kale	50
3 - Wraps & Burgers	51
Vata - Tuna and Tahini Wrap	52
Pitta - Pitta Wrap with Vegetables & Avocado	54

Kapha - Hot Wrap with Red Pepper & Mustard Seed	55
Vata - Veggie Burger	57
Pitta - Veggie Burger	58
Kapha - Spicy Veggie Burger	59

4 - Omelets — 60

Vata/Pitta - Omelet with Asparagus & Avocado	61
Kapha - Omelet with Asparagus & Eggplant	63

5 - Paneer Dishes — 64

Vata/Pitta/Kapha - How to Make Paneer	65
Vata - Paneer with Baby Spinach & Asparagus	66
Vata - Avocado and Peas with Paneer	67
Pitta - Paneer with Baby Spinach & Asparagus	68
Pitta - Paneer with Asparagus & Tahini	69
Pitta - Paneer with Peas, Avocado & Tahini	70
Kapha - Paneer with Baby Spinach & Asparagus	71
Kapha - Paneer with Eggplant, Asparagus and Hot Kapha Spice & Seed Mix	72
Kapha - Paneer with Baby Spinach & Asparagus	73

6 - Main Meals — 74

Vata - Mung Beans with Vegetables	75
Vata - Tuna and Tahini	76
Pitta - French Lentils with Vegetables	77
Pitta - Stew with French Lentils & Vegetables	78
Pitta - Stew with Asparagus & Paneer	79
Vata/Pitta/Kapha - Pan-Fried Chicken in Ghee	80
Kapha - Stew with Black Bean & Kale	81
Kapha - Brown Lentils with Vegetables	82
Kapha - Spicy Eggplant & Kale	83
Vata/Pitta/Kapha - Lassi	84
Vata/Pitta/Kapha - White Basmati Rice	85
Vata/Pitta/Kapha - Roast Potatoes with Ghee	86
Vata/Pitta/Kapha - Dhal	87
Vata/Pitta/Kapha - Quinoa	88
Vata/Pitta/Kapha - Pan-Fried Chicken in Ghee	89
Vata/Pitta - Nut Roast with Walnuts	90
Vata/Pitta/Kapha - Kitchari	92
Vata - Stew with Asparagus, Zucchini & Tahini	93

7 - Desserts — 94

Vata/Pitta - Custard	95
Pitta - Rice Pudding	96
Vata - Rice Pudding	98
Kapha - Rice Pudding	100
Vata - Pear Crumble	101
Pitta - Apple Crumble	102

    Pitta - Stewed Fig & Raisin   103

8 - Cakes   104

    Vata - Date & Walnut Cake   105
    Vata/Pitta - Fig Cake   107
    Vata/Pitta - Cherry & Almond Cake   108
    Pitta - Coconut Cake   109
    Pitta - Date Cake   110
    Kapha - Spicy Apricot Cake   111

9 - Chutneys   112

    Vata - Mango Chutney   113
    Pitta - Avocado & Walnut Chutney   114
    Kapha - Apple & Apricot Chutney   115

10 - Beverages   116

Six Complete Meals   117

Appendix I   119

Appendix II   120

1

Introduction to Ayurveda

Ayurveda means the science of life and longevity. The word comes from the Sanskrit "Veda," meaning knowledge or science, and "ayu," life. Ayurveda originated in India thousands of years ago when the rishis, or seers, first perceived this science of life while exploring the transcendental field of all the laws of nature that structures and governs the universe. Let me explain.

Many physicists think that everything we perceive on the surface level of life comes from one unified field. They even refer to it as the unified field of all the laws of nature. Confirmation of this field comes from String Theory, a theory of physics that has much more recently demonstrated how the universe consists of innumerable unmanifest virtual vibrations, laws of nature, which make up everything in creation including the human mind and body.

Some of these physicists think that there are similarities between the unified field of all the laws of nature and the field of consciousness. This might be an unfamiliar term, but it was so named by great rishis of the past because as a field, it permeates everything in creation, even the most minute particles.

For these ancient rishis, everything is born from consciousness. Such an unbounded state of consciousness, a state that not only gives rise to creation but by inference, governs and structures every part of it, is a state of deep peace and fulfillment. The rishis who experienced it within themselves, realized that the same laws of nature that structure the universe, including the plants we eat, also structure the body.

Ayurveda explains how we can thrive by maintaining harmony and balance with the laws of nature. It describes three major categories of nature's functioning so that just by identifying each person's natural mental and physical type, it is possible to determine which foods and activities he or she should favor, which to avoid, and how to maintain balance during changing seasonal influences. On that basis, Ayurveda is able to offer simple rules to follow based on our mind-body type. It often happens that, once we learn our mind-body type, the knowledge seems to resonate with who we know we are. We feel that "Yes, that's me, and I do love these recommendations."

For Ayurveda, any vulnerability from an imbalance is the root cause of disease, as it creates a weak spot in the system where disease will take hold. Thus, restoring balance is the basis of prevention and cure. Food prepared using Ayurvedic principles is the key to good health, as it serves to bring the mind-body back into balance and restore vibrant health and vitality to the whole system.

I am sharing these recipes so that you may enjoy delicious food and greater health and happiness in everything you do.

2

Ayurveda and the Three Doshas

According to Ayurveda, the many forces and laws of nature can be understood and handled in a very practical way when understood as the fundamental controlling principles found throughout nature including the physiology and food. These three controlling principles are called Doshas. Everything in the universe is governed by them and they interact through innumerable laws of nature, or impulses of intelligence, so that all life functions with intelligence. We each have a unique blend of these doshas which determines our nature.

When we are in balance, these three principles, Vata, Pitta, and Kapha, act together to support a healthy mind and body. When we are out of balance, through improper diet or fatigue, for example, we become vulnerable to dis-ease, which can cause health issues. Essentially, any weak point in the body will be the site of imbalance, and can be exploited by impurities or foreign organisms, which take the opportunity to grow.

Meet the Three Doshas: Vata, Pitta, Kapha

These three controlling principles are easy to understand and to see in all aspects of life.

Dosha	Function	Elements	Times of Year
Vata	Movement	Space and Air	Winter, Early Spring and Late Autumn
Pitta	Transformation	Fire and Water	Summer and Early Autumn
Kapha	Structure	Water and Earth	Spring

Now, let's look at these three in more practical detail by taking a mind-body questionnaire that will reveal exactly how the abstract qualities of Vata, Pitta, and Kapha appear in our own lives. I am sure that you will readily recognize yourself, including any personal likes and dislikes that you may not have even noticed before. I have given this questionnaire to well over 1,500 people, and the overwhelming response is that the characteristics that they reveal prove to be an accurate description of (you) themselves. With your results in hand, you will be able to choose the right recipes for your mind-body type.

	VATA (V)	PITTA (P)	KAPHA (K)
What is your body type?	○ Lean, thin	○ Moderate build	○ A little heavy
What is your speaking style?	○ Fast-paced & likes to talk	○ Moderately-paced	○ Slower speaker
How is your appetite & thirst?	○ Irregular appetite	○ Strong appetite & strong thirst	○ Lighter appetite & moderate thirst
How is your usual digestion?	○ Smaller quantities	○ Strong digestion	○ Digestion can be weak
How regular are you?	○ Sometimes a little irregular	○ Regular & tendency towards loose stools	○ Regular
What are your food preferences?	○ Likes sweet, salty & sour foods	○ Likes sweet & bitter foods	○ Likes spicy, astringent & pungent foods
How is your memory?	○ Quick to memorize, but tendency to forget	○ Moderate memory	○ Slow to learn but good long term memory
How are your sleep patterns?	○ Can experience disturbed sleep	○ Moderate sleep	○ Easy & deep, sound sleep
What activities do you enjoy?	○ Likes arts, music, dance & travel	○ Likes problem solving & competitive sports	○ Likes sports requiring stamina e.g. football
What type of personality are you?	○ Creative, friendly, imaginative, can rush a little	○ Determined, ambitious, confident, usually charming & focused	○ Well-grounded, truthful, loyal, patient & usually satisfied in life
TOTALS (add up ticks)			

Understanding Your Mind-Body Type

Most of us have both a predominant and a secondary dosha. Pitta may predominate with Vata a close second, and Kapha not so much, or one might have Vata predominating, and the other two not so much. Or your score could look like this, for example: V-5, P-3, K-2, indicating a Vata/Pitta type. When just one dosha is your predominating characteristic, the second and third scores would be less than 2, like this: V8, P-1, K-1. This would be interpreted as just Vata, but this occurs very rarely, for maybe 1 in 100. Another rarity is to score equally on all three doshas.

Your unique mind-body type influences you physically, mentally, and emotionally. To understand your score, read about the qualities of Vata, Pitta, and Kapha to see which apply to you. Because Ayurveda considers the basis of good health to be balanced doshas, you will want to know which doshas you most need to balance when you plan your meals. There is a good reason for this. Unsuitable diets, routine, and too much stress produce imbalance in the mind and body. Understanding the doshas will help you to restore and maintain balance in mind and body.

An overview of the qualities of each dosha

General Qualities	Vata	Pitta	Kapha
Structure	Bony, thin, quick moving	Well proportioned, often muscular	Well formed, big build, strong muscles
Body Weight	Naturally slim	Medium Build	Larger frame and solid, heavier
Complexion	Cold, dry	Warm, light, sightly oily, sweats easily, prone to moles or freckles	Thick skin, can be oily
Thirst	Varied	Can be excessive	Moderate
Mental Traits	Creative, imaginative, quick thinking, changeable, easy going	Focused, goal orientated, assertive, often leads, intellectual	Steady, reliable, slow, loyal
Memory and Concentration	Quick to learn, good short-term memory, longer term not so good	Moderate learning time, generally good memory	Slow to learn but remembers very well
General Personality	Enthusiastic, uncertain, tends to worry	Sharp minded, can be critical, confident	Steady and reliable, even tempered, loyal
Sleep	Light and often interrupted	Average time of sleep sufficient, usually sound sleep	Heavy sleeper, can be hard to rouse.

It makes sense to bring your three doshas back into balance by choosing a suitable diet and routine.

In Ayurveda, there are two aspects to consider for health your underlying: the dosha pattern, which is your nature, which is called your Prakriti, and the dosha imbalance. This reflects how you have deviated from your true nature and is called your Vikriti. In practice, these terms "Prakriti" and "Vikriti" are not our concern when looking at the questionnaire result. It only serves as a current and accurate reflection of what you need to balance. With improved balance, your score may change somewhat. Perhaps a very high Vata reading will settle down. But in my experience, the change tends not to be radical enough to change your mind-body type score.

The Doshas at Work in the Mind-Body

Vata

Vata, movement, governs:

- The circulation of the blood
- The signals that move along the nerves to transmit information, temperature or pain
- All movement, including the simple act of walking and all muscle movement involved

When out of balance, Vata types are especially vulnerable to:

- Mental: Anxiety and memory loss, panic, phobia, insomnia, hyperactivity, and attention deficit disorder
- Physical: Variable digestion, constipation, irritable bowel syndrome, palpitations, and osteoarthritis
- Cold hands and feet

Remember that Vata, Pitta, and Kapha are subtle qualities, but they can be readily identified in life.

Vata:

Qualities are:

- Quick, light, dry, rough, and cold
- Personality is creative, lively, erratic
- Bodily location is said to be seated in the colon
- Vata dominant times of day are 2 to 6 am and 2 to 6 pm
- Vata dominant season is winter and late autumn
- Vata dominant time of life is over age 60

Pitta

Pitta, transformation, governs:

- The digestive system, transforming food into nutrients for the cells in the body
- The transformation processes in intellectual thought
- Health processes

When out of balance, Pitta types are vulnerable to:

- Mental: Impatience, anger, guilt, obsessive behavior patterns, and can be aggressive, domineering
- Physical: Ulcers, hepatitis, inflammation, hemorrhoids, colitis, cystitis, and dermatitis

Pitta:

Qualities are:

- Sharp, bright, warm/hot
- Personality is focused, ambitious, competitive, and they tend to be leaders
- Location is said to be seated in the stomach and small intestine
- Pitta dominant times of day are 10 am to 2 pm and 10 pm to 2 am
- Pitta dominant season is Summer and early autumn
- Pitta dominant time of life is about age 30 to 60

Kapha

Kapha, structure, governs:

- The bones and the bodily structures
- The mental structures, such as the brain, the spinal canal, and so forth, which uphold the planning and organizing of activity

When out of balance, Kapha types are vulnerable to:

- Mental: Depression, greed, lack of motivation, and lethargy
- Physical: Weak digestion, obesity, high cholesterol, hypothyroid, type 2 diabetes, and sinusitis, oily hair and skin

Kapha:

Qualities are:

- Slow, heavy, cold, wet, and stable
- Personality is consistent, compassionate, stable, and reliable
- Location in the body is seated in the upper chest and neck
- Kapha dominant times of day are 6 am to 10 am and 6 pm to 10 pm
- Kapha dominant season is spring
- Kapha dominant time of life is about from birth to age 30

You may have noticed by now that Kapha types tend to be of bigger build, thus, vigorous movement is good for them. The Kapha time of life, birth to age 30, includes the early years of childhood, when growing children like to run around a lot, and it is now well known that plenty of exercise in childhood is fundamental to the proper formation of the bones of young children. For Kapha mind-body types, movement and exercise are essential for staying balanced and in good form, at all times of life. Later in life exercise levels may be reduced a little, but still need to be more for a Kapha than for a Vata or Pitta type.

Ayurveda makes personalized recommendations for just what kind of exercise and recreation Vata, Pitta, and Kapha types need, and how much and even at what time of day and season. However, this book places special importance on food.

Your kitchen is your pharmacopoeia, and your culinary habits can be the foundation for good health and happiness. They can empower you to maintain good health and vitality all year round.

The six tastes and the doshas:

- Vata is balanced by salty, sweet, and sour tastes
- Pitta is balanced by sweet, bitter, and astringent
- Kapha is balanced by bitter, astringent, and pungent

It is important at this stage to remember that most people have one mind-body type predominant and one secondary. Kapha/Pitta types, for example, enjoy spicy foods and bitter and astringent tastes, such as basil and apples. But because these types are secondarily Pitta dosha, they're also likely to enjoy some sweet foods, such as rice pudding and grapes.

Knowing that tastes affect our doshas, Vata, Pitta, and Kapha, which are naturally expressed in us mentally, emotionally, and physically, we can make better conscious choices when we plan our meals. We can greatly influence and support our health, emotions, and behavior simply through the sense of taste.

3

How to Create Balance Using the Six Tastes

Ayurveda explains that to feel satisfied after a meal, it is important to include all six tastes. Only then will the body feel that the need for food has been met, and the attention be able to shift onto something other than food. If you do not have all six tastes, you may want to continue eating even when you are no longer hungry in an attempt to find the missing taste. This type of overeating can lead to being overweight. Clearly, one cannot always include all six tastes pleasingly in all dishes, like rice pudding, for example. But if you can include all six in the meal, I can assure you that it will help prevent putting on those extra pounds. Moreover, the satisfaction of having included all six tastes will allow you to focus fully on your after-meal activities, without being distracted by the craving for a nibble. A very suitable option is to ensure that all six tastes are at least present in every day's food intake.

Now you can take into account your mind-body type to know which of the six tastes should predominate in your meal. Most people have both a predominant and a secondary type, such as Kapha/Pitta. If you are this type, you may like to use some of the fruits or vegetables that are listed as best for you, and you at least can see which fruits or vegetables are best to avoid. Do not worry. Some ingredients are very good for Pitta types and not good for purely Kapha types, but a Kapha/Pitta person, with Kapha foremost, should simply be aware that sweet foods to balance Pitta are required from time to time, but focusing on tastes that balance Kapha should be primary.

The six tastes appeal to the body and the mind, and these affect our food preferences. With a little knowledge of Ayurveda, you will soon find that you naturally select what you want to eat more regularly, in accord with the balance in nature's intelligence.

The table below shows the tastes related to each dosha.

Taste	Heating/Cooling	Balances	Examples
Sweet	Cooling	Vata/Pitta	Banana, milk, rice, wheat, sweet potato, cauliflower
Sour	Heating	Vata	Pineapple, strawberry, lemon
Salty	Heating	Vata	Salt
Bitter	Heating	Pitta/Kapha	Green vegetables including chard, chocolate
Astringent	Cooling	Pitta/Kapha	Apples, lentils, beans, honey
Pungent	Cooling	Kapha	Cayenne pepper, paprika, black pepper, ginger

Taste is how we balance ourselves, and below is a list of foods that balances each type.

Vata Pacifying Foods

In general, Vata types should favor foods that are warm, oily, heavy, sweet, sour, or salty. Limit foods that are cold, dry, light, pungent, bitter, or astringent. More specifically, choose foods from the following list.

Dairy Products—All dairy products pacify Vata but avoid taking milk with a full meal. Cheese should ideally be soft and fresh, not aged.

Fruits—Favor sweet and heavy fruits, such as avocados, grapes, cherries, pears, peaches, melons, berries, plums, bananas, sweet oranges, pineapples, mangoes, figs, and papayas. Limit dry or light fruits, such as apples, pears, pomegranates, cranberries, and dried fruits. Soak dried fruits in warm water to reduce the Vata-aggravating properties. Dates are best taken with ghee.

Sweeteners—All sweeteners pacify Vata but should not be taken in excess. Honey should be cold pressed because heating damages its nutritional properties. According to Ayurveda, honey is unsuitable when it has been heated.

Beans—Limit all beans except for mung dhal and tofu (soybean curd).

Nuts—All nuts are good for balancing Vata.

Grains—Rice and wheat are good, but reduce barley, corn, millet, buckwheat, rye, and oats.

Oils—All oils are good.

Spices—Cardamom, cumin, ginger, cinnamon, salt, cloves, mustard seed, and small quantities of black pepper are beneficial.

Vegetables—Beets, carrots, asparagus, cucumbers, and sweet potatoes, are best cooked but do not eat raw.

Vegetables suitable in moderation—Peas, green leafy vegetables, broccoli, cauliflower, celery, zucchini (courgettes), and spinach (small quantity) if cooked, especially with ghee (clarified butter). It is best to avoid sprouts and cabbage.

Pitta Pacifying Foods

In general, favor foods that are heavy, oily, sweet, bitter, or astringent. Minimize foods that are hot, light, dry, pungent, sour, or salty. More specifically, choose from among the following.

Dairy Products—Ghee (clarified butter), milk, cream, and cream cheese are good for pacifying Pitta. Minimize aged cheeses, salted butter, and sour milk products, like yogurt.

Fruits—Sweet fruits are good, such as apples, grapes, pomegranates, figs, bananas, avocados, and mangoes. Limit sour fruits.

Sweeteners—White or semi-refined sugar is good for pacifying Pitta but not in excess. Limit molasses and brown sugar. Honey can be taken in small quantities.

Beans—Mung dal and soybeans are good.

Nuts—Limit all nuts, except coconut.

Grains—Wheat, rice, barley, and oats are good. Limit millet, corn, buckwheat, and rye.

Oils—Ghee is best for pacifying Pitta dosha.

Spices—Coriander, cumin, ginger in small amounts, turmeric, saffron, fennel, cinnamon, and cardamom are good. Reduce pepper, mustard seeds, cloves, and chillies.

Vegetables—Asparagus, zucchini (courgettes), cauliflower, broccoli, cabbage, green beans, potatoes, sweet potatoes, peas, and peppers are good. Reduce beets and carrots and avoid tomatoes.

Kapha Pacifying Foods

In general, favor foods that are light, dry, warm, pungent, bitter, or astringent. Minimize foods that are heavy, oily, cold, sweet, salty, or sour and also minimize taking large quantities of food, especially at night. Choose foods from the list below.

Dairy Products—Low-fat milk is best. Ideally, always boil milk before you drink it and take it warm. Avoid taking milk with a full meal or with sour or salty food. You can add one or two pinches of turmeric or ginger to whole milk before boiling. Limit aged cheeses and, for that matter, any other cheeses, and yogurts.

Fruits—Favor lighter fruits, such as apples and pears. Reduce heavy or sour fruits such as oranges, bananas, pineapples, figs, dates, avocados, coconuts, and melons.

Sweeteners—Honey is good but not heated. Limit products which contain sugar.

Beans—All beans are fine, except tofu (soybean curd).

Nuts—Reduce eating nuts.

Grains—Most grains are fine, especially barley and millet. Minimize eating too much wheat, rice, or oats.

Oils—Avoid all oils. Very small amounts of ghee are fine.

Spices—All spices are fine, except for salt.

Vegetables—All are fine, except tomatoes, cucumbers and sweet potatoes.

Cooking for Families and Friends with More than one Mind-body Type

To make cooking more practical for families and other social assemblies—where there are often two or sometimes three different mind-body types—a simple solution is to cook one meal and adjust for flavor by dividing the cooked vegetables into two or three groups after they have been cooked, and then adding the herbs and spices. Also, some vegetables, such as asparagus and eggplant (aubergine), are tri-doshic, which means they are suitable for all three types. Tri-doshic vegetables make great choices for any gathering.

Because Vata and Pitta are both balanced by the sweet taste, and every dish includes salt, it is easy to make a savory dish with all ingredients the same for Vata and Pitta—up to the point where you add the spices. For example, a soup or main meal could have dahl, basmati rice, quinoa, or yellow lentils for protein, and asparagus, carrots, and sweet potato for the vegetables. Then for spicing, add fresh chopped cilantro, which is suitable for both Vata and Pitta. Then simply add Vata spice mix to the Vata dish and Pitta spice mix plus coconut milk to the Pitta dish.

For Kapha types, I have often added to the same cooked vegetables, mustard seeds, paprika, ginger, black pepper, and sometimes cayenne pepper, in place of the Kapha spice mix. This is often suitable for those who are mostly Kapha first and Pitta second, so if you spice up some green vegetables, they will be fine with it. Remember, if possible, to include all six tastes in a meal to give the feeling of satisfaction. A simple solution is to add a squeeze of citrus to all dishes, apart from the sweet desserts—lemon juice for Vata types and lime for Pitta and Kapha types.

How to assimilate the food most effectively

It's not enough simply to ingest the right food. Digestion is a very complex and important function. There are three golden rules to maximize your digestive power and get the most from your meal.

- No mobile phone, no TV.
- Eat sitting down comfortably either in silence or with low volume beautiful music, or while having a pleasant conversation with family or friends.
- Sit quietly for at least five minutes after the meal to let the digestive power work its magic.

To digest and assimilate the food properly, your body redirects much of the blood flow to your stomach. If you get up too soon after a meal, the blood flow shifts to serve whatever activity you take up, be it texting a friend, walking to the kitchen, taking a walk, reading, or writing, so the digestive process becomes disturbed. You may even feel some heaviness or a little ache while walking.

Here is what the Ayurvedic text suggests you do after a meal:

Sit like a king for 5-10 minutes, walk 100 steps and lie down on your left side for about 15-20 minutes (do not fall asleep). You will become aware how your digestive system functions as your attention will be naturally drawn to your stomach. You may call this time, siesta time!

Try it for a week and see how you feel.

4
My Vata, Pitta, and Kapha Spice Mixes

My spice mixes are ready to use, so you will not have to mix them up every time you need them. They were inspired by Maharishi Ayurveda churnas, which are designed to balance Vata, Pitta, and Kapha, but one important difference is that I have excluded the sugar and salt, which will make it easier to control the amounts of these when you use my spice mixes in your cooking and even your drinks. You can add sugar or salt if and when desired in proportions that best suit the needs and tastes of the diners.

Each spice has special properties and tastes related to the doshas. Some spices suit all three doshas, while others are suitable for two mind-body types. In some cases, I added a small amount of a spice not pertinent to the main dosha that the mix is intended to balance, but the quantity is so low that the overall mix still serves to balance the dosha after which a spice mix is named. My spice mix recipes take into account a mix of two predominant doshas; moreover, the beneficial properties of certain spices are well worth including in small amounts due to their beneficial properties. I kept this in mind while developing my recipes.

I use coriander in all the mixes because of its beneficial effects and because it is tri-doshic, suitable for all mind-body types. So, in some meals you can opt for cooking with fresh chopped cilantro, if that is seasonally available, instead of coriander powder. Many of the recipes here even specify cilantro as an option. When using fresh cilantro in this way, it is appropriate to put more into a meal than the powdered coriander. Typically, a dish for three people tastes best with ⅛ of a cup (10 to 15 g) of cilantro.

Finally, chop the cilantro and then boil it in a little water until the water all boils off. Set aside while you sauté the other spices in ghee. Sautéing the spices releases the flavors and their medicinal properties for a fuller, more beneficial taste. Then add the cilantro to the spices and mix them into the cooked vegetables. Once everything else is ready, weigh the vegetables to determine just the right amount of salt required—0.5% of the total weight. With a little practice, this procedure becomes second nature.

For soups, you can blend all the vegetables to obtain a creamy texture. Alternatively, blend just a half or one third of the vegetables.

The spice mixes work well for savory dishes. Still, you may prefer to use herbs along with the spices—or instead of the spices. One example of this is nut roast, which benefits from Italian seasoning—a mix of four parts basil, two parts oregano, and one part thyme. The recipes specify a variety of such variations.

The table below shows the ingredients used in each mix with their tastes and some of their benefits.

Key: V = Vata, P = Pitta, and K = Kapha.

Spice	Doshas	Tastes	Doshas it Balances	Benefits and Uses
Cinnamon	VPK	sweet, pungent, bitter	VK	Improves digestion. Increases circulation and is good for the central nervous system. Purifies the blood.
Coriander	VPK	sweet, astringent	VPK	Purifies the blood. Alleviates urinary tract infection and constipation.
Cardamom	VPK	sweet, pungent	VPK	Excellent digestive aid. Lowers blood pressure. Clears sinuses.
Cumin	VPK	bitter, pungent	VPK	Aids digestion. Helps flush toxins.
Ginger	VPK	pungent, sweet, bitter	VPK (Use less for Pitta.)	Excellent digestive aid. Improves assimilation of food.
Turmeric	PK	pungent, bitter, mildly astringent	PK	Reduces weight gain. Very good for the skin and complexion.
Fennel	PV	sweet, bitter	VP	Enhances the digestive fire without increasing Pitta. Good for the intellect and the eyes. Antioxidant.
Black Pepper	VK	pungent	KV	Cleanser.

Recipes for the Spice Mixes

Vata Mix	Oz	%
Cinnamon	12.63	39.5%
Coriander	8.42	26.3%
Cardamom	3.37	10.5%
Cumin	3.37	10.5%
Ginger	2.53	7.9%
Turmeric	1.68	5.3%
Total	**32.00**	

Pitta Mix	Oz	%
Fennel	12.97	40.5%
Coriander	8.65	27.0%
Cardamom	2.59	8.1%
Cumin	2.59	8.1%
Ginger	1.73	5.4%
Turmeric	1.73	5.4%
Cinnamon	1.73	5.4%
Total	**32.00**	

Kapha Mix	Oz	%
Ginger	12.08	37.7%
Cumin	7.25	22.6%
Coriander	7.25	22.6%
Turmeric	2.42	7.5%
Cinnamon	2.42	7.5%
Black Pepper	0.60	1.9%
Total	**32.00**	

HOT KAPHA SEED MIX

Hot Kapha Seed Mix	20 oz Jar	%
Mustard Seeds	14	70
Cumin Seeds	6	30
Total		**100**

Hot Kapha Spice Mix	5 oz Jar	%
Paprika	105.0	70
Ginger	27.0	18
Cayenne Pepper	10.5	7
Black Pepper	7.5	5
Total	150	100

Hot Kapha Seed Mix		80
Hot Kapha Spice Mix		20

Proposed proportion of each mix to add to foods. I recommend 1 parts of spice mix to 4 parts of seed mix. Once you have experience with these you may want to use your own proportions.

5

Introduction to the Recipes

The recipes that follow are laid out in a way that makes it simple to find what you need to suit the guests and the occasion. For instance, each recipe's title shows which dosha types the dish is designed to balance. In some cases, the recipe for Vata and Pitta is identical, apart from the addition of lemon or lime, the suitable dosha mix, or other ingredients, like ginger. The recipes will specify how to add these dosha-specific options. If there is more than one mind-body type being served—as is most common—you can save time by dividing the cooked vegetables into two or three dishes, one for each dosha type, before adding the spices and other dosha-specific ingredients. It's usually quite simple. If out of four vegetables one is not ideal for someone, then adding the suitable spices and herbs will neutralize its effect. You might, for example, have a recipe for soup with asparagus, eggplant (aubergine), and zucchini that includes cauliflower, which is better for Pitta, or carrots, which are better for Vata, and then balance their effects with the right spice mixes, as needed. This is one way to resolve a potentially tricky problem for the cook.

Ghee

Vegans may replace ghee with sunflower or olive oil. Ghee is clarified butter with the milk solids removed in a simple process which results in a substance so pure that it resists spoiling, even when not kept in the refrigerator. Ghee can often replace butter in cooking but is more easily digestible. Also, unlike butter, ghee can withstand high temperatures during cooking without burning. This unctuous food helps to ease the flow of nutrients throughout the body and into the cells, transport waste from the cells, and eliminate it from the body. Ghee enhances the digestive fire and so aids in the assimilation of food. In Ayurveda, ghee is much used as it is considered tridoshic and therefore valuable for preparing foods. Kapha types, who already contain this oily quality in their constitutions, should limit their intake of ghee.

Sweeteners

White sugar and raw cane sugar are highly processed, and Ayurveda recommends using alternatives. Here are some sugar alternatives I have used to sweeten my recipes:

Coconut sugar—1 cup of coconut sugar equals 1 cup of cane sugar in both volume and sweetness, and they have similar textures. This means that the finished product will be similar.

Monk fruit—150 to 200 times sweeter than sugar. If a monk fruit product is pure and unmixed with other substances, then use ¾ of a teaspoon of monk fruit in place of 1 cup of white cane sugar. Otherwise, follow the equivalency given on the product package.

Date or raisin pulp—Soaked, cooked, and blended, these may not taste like sugar, but they do lend a special sweetness and taste of their own. They work especially well in rice pudding. Or in a stewed pear, yogurt and Vata spice mix dish, adding blended raisins, vanilla essence, cardamom, and a squeeze of lemon juice (optional) to the yogurt results in a truly delicious treat.

The recipes in this book call for coconut sugar, but you can substitute whatever sweetener you wish. I designed a few recipes to be specifically sugar free. These will be of special interest to anyone seeking to address gut imbalances, which are linked to excess sugar intake.

The Gut Issue

The gut—your intestinal system, which includes the digestive microbes that live there—plays a key role in maintaining vibrant health. This is where most of the digestive process takes place. For many, this foundation of our vitality may be in need of repair and rejuvenation. Physiologist Robert Keith Wallace discusses how, when the system has become inefficient and even detrimental to well-being, a simple regimen can transform the adverse conditions in this essential organ. In his book, *The Rest and Repair Diet,* he recommends a three-week diet that excludes sugar, gluten (found in wheat), and dairy in order to reset the intestinal microbiome. He explains how the gut bacteria communicate directly with the brain. If unfavorable bacteria have overrun the intestinal ecology, these unwelcome guests can issue a demand for sugar. The brain receives the message that you, the host, need some sugar. You now have a sugar craving. But you and your brain are not aware that the message is coming from the bacteria and does not actually speak for the needs of your body. Dr. Wallace's three-week gut repair diet is designed to reconfigure your intestinal ecology by starving out the bad bacteria and setting up favorable conditions for the ones that speak for our well-being. After the diet, many people notice an increased sensitivity to sugars and a reduced desire for sweets. In support of this laudable effort, I have included several sugar-free desserts among my recipes.

Salt

Traditional wisdom holds that a savory main dish should include one half of a percent of salt. As you follow the recipes, you will quite likely notice that the amount of each raw ingredient you add does not come out after cooking to be exactly the same volume as the amount called for in the recipe. So in the end, you need to determine how much you have so you can calculate the one half of a percent of salt that you need to add in order to finish the dish. It is also possible to add salt to taste, and simply try the food, but knowing how much the dish would normally weigh does help. Getting the salt right is one practical reason why getting yourself a good food kitchen scale is essential.

Herb Mix 1 and Desert Mix 1

My recipes do not always use just Vata, Pitta, or Kapha spice mixes. A few recipes also include—or substitute—special sweet or savory mixes, which I call Desert Mix1 and Herb Mix 1. You can concoct a small supply of these mixes yourself and have them ready to use when you need them. Prepare them in the following proportions:

Herb Mix 1

		oz	%
Dried Basil	⅔ cup	⅔	57%
Oregano	⅓ cup	⅓	28.5%
Thyme	2 Tbsp	⅙	14%

Use this as an alternative to Italian seasoning. Just substitute the same amount of this mix in any recipe.

A savory recipe might ask for ½ oz (15g) of Herb Mix 1.

Dessert Mix 1

To create a quick and simple treat, I often use this mix:

		oz	%
Cardamom	1 cup	4	80%
Nutmeg (fresh)	¼ cup	1	20%

A sweet recipe could ask for a tablespoon of Dessert Mix 1.

My Flexible Favorites—to Accommodate All Your Guests

Certain ingredients appear in quite a few of the recipes in this book. This is because their qualities make them either suitable for all three of the mind-body types, Vata, Pitta, and Kapha, or readily adaptable to suit all three doshas. For example, while Zucchini is not ideal for Kapha types, a small quantity in a suitably spiced meal poses no problem. This approach is especially effective because approximately 999 people out of a 1,000 have one predominant dosha plus a secondary one. This means that a little spice or food that balances the secondary dosha—but not the primary one—will be not only alright, but actually beneficial to the constitution and pleasing to the taste. Here are a few of my favorite ingredients for making a meal work for all your friends and family.

Asparagus

A fortunate blend of sweet, bitter, and astringent tastes makes asparagus a truly tri-doshic vegetable. It is one of the very few foods in the world that naturally balances all three doshas. Also a great diuretic, asparagus is especially healthy for the urinary tract. The pleasingly unique taste of asparagus combines well with a wide array of foods for creating delicious savory dishes.

Avocado

Avocado is one of the most popular vegetables on the table. Rich in the healthy fats we need, avocado supplies them in easily digestible form and so is especially beneficial for those who have difficulty digesting fats. Avocado increases Kapha and decreases Vata and Pitta. Kapha/Pitta types especially tend to like it, and it soothes Vata dosha. Avocado's subtly delicious taste and creamy texture make it a welcome addition to soups and stews to make a thicker, richer dish.

Cilantro and Ground Coriander

Cilantro, the leaf of the coriander plant, serves as a wonderful digestive without adding heat. Thus, it balances all three doshas and is especially valuable for Pitta people. Cilantro can be chopped and mixed with yogurt and water to make lassi, a pleasing digestive drink. A wonderful aromatic, cilantro's complex taste blends sweet, bitter, astringent, and a little pungent. It is best served cooked and goes well with other herbs and spices.

Ground coriander comes from the seed of the coriander plant and serves the same doshic properties as leafy cilantro. The taste, however, differs somewhat; cilantro offers a fresh, slightly citrusy taste and smell, while coriander's is subtly warmer, nuttier, and spicier. Luckily, those who do not like cilantro can still appreciate coriander. Some of the recipes in this book specify how to substitute one for the other to suit preference and availability. You can make your own substitutions as you wish. Just keep in mind that a quarter of a cup of chopped cilantro (25 g) is interchangeable with a tablespoon (5 g) of ground coriander.

Take note, however, that it is not really necessary to substitute anything whenever cilantro must be left out of the dish for any reason. Even without it, the balancing effect will still work, since the other ingredients in the recipe provide tastes that give the same effect. So, even though cilantro contributes a nice freshness to the dish, if the leafy herb is unavailable, it is not essential to add anything in its place.

Ginger

Ayurveda calls this tuber, which is famous for aiding digestion, the universal medicine because all health depends on the vitality of the digestive fire. Ginger not only has been known from antiquity to be one of the main foods and spices that strengthen the digestive fire, but also has been found by modern scientific research to be a very effective tonic for both indigestion and motion sickness. Ayurvedic physicians make a paste with powdered ginger for treating headaches and toothaches. An analgesic, ginger increases bioavailability and so enhances the beneficial effects of all that we take into the body, making it excellent for the respiratory system and, of course, digestion. Adding ginger to a dish is an Ayurvedic way to make your food not only delicious, but also your best medicine. Pitta dominant people should be moderate with ginger, because of its heating effect.

Lemon and Lime

These citrus fruits are famous for their appetizing effects. Add a squeeze or a spoonful of these zesty sours to lend a satisfying complexity to a dish that both piques the appetite and enhances the digestion. Because sour taste helps to kindle the digestive fire, tradition holds that loss of appetite calls for a bite of lemon with a little salt to stimulate the appetite. Lime is less sour and therefore more cooling than lemon, and so is a bit better than lemon for Pitta and Kapha types.

Zucchini

This late-summer squash is both nourishing and easy to digest. It is good for both Vata and Pitta people and has a neutral effect for Kapha people. Zucchini is also especially suitable for those with weak digestion. Small adjustments in seasoning will easily optimize its value for any dosha, making zucchini a welcome addition to many dishes.

For Vegans

Vegans will certainly want to avoid ghee, as it is a milk product. Just substitute ghee with sunflower oil or olive oil.

Getting the Essential Amino Acids

There are nine essential amino acids—essential because they must all be included in our daily diet to build the proteins we need. Knowing how to include them all in a meal in order to get complete protein is important for everyone, but especially for vegetarians and those who want to introduce healthy vegetarian dishes into their diet. Among my recipes, those that include quinoa, rice and dahl, or lentils provide all nine of the essential amino acids.

Equipment

Here are some tried and true tools I use for ease and accuracy of preparation and for best results.

Kitchen scale. Get a good one, with ounce and gram display with readings that are accurate within one tenth of a gram.

Steamer Pot.

Blender. I like a Vita Mix, which can blend hot foods as well as cold, but there are many good brands available. You will use it to blend about one third of a soup very finely to give it a nice texture. A good blender will also process nuts and seeds.

Food processor. These can be good for cakes but are not needed as often.

Mincer. Designed for mincing meats, this tool works well for processing dried fruits. There are manual versions, but I recommend an electric one for much greater ease when preparing tougher ingredients like dried apricots.

Nutri-bullet® juicer. This is useful for quick-blending soups and smoothies.

Watch for New Recipes, Coming Soon

This cookbook is enough to get you started with a healthy range of recipes for different occasions and people, but the story does not end there. I will be sharing new recipes on a regular basis on my website, AyurvedaEasyTransformation.com. Pay us a visit to find out more. Not everything would fit in this cookbook, so quite a few food favorites that have been left out will soon start to show up online. So, save room for more. You'll find more recipes for pasta like spaghetti or rice noodles, and paneer pizza and mung dahl pancakes, a nutritional powerhouse, as well as a variety of cookies, and more. Meanwhile, I hope you will enjoy preparing the dishes that follow.

A Final Note

While each recipe specifies how much of the spice mixes to add, you will no doubt find that some like a more generous dusting of their favorites. Feel free to adjust the quantities of spice mixes to suit the tastes of your guests. An easy way to please everyone would be to just follow the recipe and then place containers of the most-favored spice mixes on the dinner table. Then guests can have an extra sprinkle on their meals, as they please.

I hope you enjoy preparing these recipes and sharing the results with your guests.

1

Breakfast

The breakfast in this section offers a small range of recipes to give a brief outlook of what's available for Vata, Pitta and Kapha. The three Vata, Pitta and Kapha spreads are ideal on toast or crackers for breakfast or for a snack at any time of day. Cereals can be adjusted for each type with a sprinkling of the appropriate Spice Mix as well as nuts and seeds, including: almonds for Vata types, sunflower and pumpkin seeds for Pitta types and honey for Kapha because nuts are not as suitable for Kapha types. Also, since most people are a mix of two types, many will want to mix and match these ingredients. For example, Kapha/Pitta types may from time to time especially want to balance Pitta with stewed apple with raisins and honey, or pumpkin seeds. Fruit salads also make a nice breakfast treat. I offer just a few recipes for breakfast here, but with all these options, there are so many possibilities. I am posting more great breakfast recipes on the website on a regular basis. You will find them at: AyurvedaEasyTransformation.com

Vata/Pitta

Oatmeal

🕐 20 minutes   🍴 Serves 2

STEP 1

- ⅔ cup (50 g) quick oats
- 2½ cups (625 g) milk

STEP 2

For Vata:

- ½ cup (60 g) ground or flaked almonds
- 2 Tbsp (20 g) coconut sugar, or to taste
- 2 tsp (4 g) cardamom
- ½ tsp (1 g) nutmeg, grated

For Pitta:

- 1 Tbsp (7 g) Pitta Spice Mix – or to taste
- ¼ cup (30 g) ground pumpkin seeds
- 2 Tbsp (20 g) coconut sugar – or to taste
- ½ cup (45 g) desiccated coconut

PREPARATION

1. Add the milk and the oats to a pot over high heat and stir for 4-5 minutes. Then reduce to medium heat and simmer for 10 – 15 more minutes, until the oats have become soft. If you want a quicker cooking time, blend the oats into a flour and cooking time is reduced by about 10 minutes.
2. Add the ingredients for the appropriate type in Step 2 and continue to stir for 3-4 minutes.

Kapha

Oatmeal

🕐 15 minutes 🍴 Serves 2

STEP 1

- ⅔ cup (50 g) quick oats
- 2½ cups (625 g) water

STEP 2

- 1 Tbsp (8 g) Hot Kapha Seed Mix
- 1 tsp (2.5 g) Hot Kapha Spice Mix – or to taste
- 2 Tbsp (20 g) sunflower seeds
- 1 Tbsp (15 g) honey – or to taste

PREPARATION

1. Add the water and the oats to a pan on a high heat and stir for 4-5 minutes. Then reduce to a medium heat and simmer for 5 more minutes.
2. Add the ingredients for the appropriate type, in Step 2 and continue to stir for 3-4 minutes. Add the honey after the porridge has cooled to a warm temperature, under 40°C. The nutritional properties of honey are impaired when it is heated above 40°C.

Pitta

Stewed Apples

🕐 10 minutes 🍴 Serves 2

STEP 1

- 4 cups (360 g) 2 large apples, peeled and chopped into medium sized pieces
- ½ cup (60 g) raisins, stewed

STEP 2

- ⅔ (140 g) coconut milk
- 1 Tbsp (7 g) Allspice
- 2 tsp (3.5 g) cardamom
- ½ Tbsp (7 g) ghee (optional)

PREPARATION

1. Add the chopped apples and the raisins to 2 cups of water in a large pan over high heat. When the water is boiling, reduce to medium heat and cook for 5-10 minutes until tender. Drain off all the water.
2. Mix in the Allspice, cardamom, coconut milk, and ghee.

Pitta

Stewed Apple with Raisins & Coconut

🕐 10 minutes 🍴 Serves 2

STEP 1

- 4 cups (360 g) 2 large apples, peeled and chopped into medium sized pieces
- ½ cup (60 g) raisins, soaked

STEP 2

- ⅔ cup (140 g) coconut milk
- 1 cup (40 g) desiccated coconut
- 3 Tbsp (21 g) Pitta Spice Mix
- Optionally add ¼ cup (30 g) ground almonds
- 1 Tbsp (15 g) ghee (optional)
- 2 tsp (8 g) lime juice – or to taste
- ¾ tsp (3 g) salt – or to taste

PREPARATION

1. Add the chopped apples and the raisins to 2 cups of water in a large pan over medium heat. When the water is boiling, reduce to medium heat and cook for about 5 minutes.
2. Add all the other ingredients and change to a low heat and cook for a further 10 minutes or until the apples are tender. While cooking it may be suitable to add more water if required.

Vata

Almond Spread

🕐 10 minutes   🍴 Serves 2 cups

A great tasting almond spread with a tangy flavor.

STEP 1

- 1½ cups and 1 Tbsp (380g) Almond Butter
- ¾ cup (72 g) Vata Spice Mix
- 2½ Tbsp (24 g) coconut sugar
- ½ tsp (2.4 g) salt

PREPARATION

1. Weigh out all the ingredients and mix thoroughly.

Pitta

Sunflower Spread

🕐 10 minutes   🍴 Serves 2 Cups

A great tasting sunflower spread with a sweet flavor.

STEP 1

- 1½ cups (384 g) Pitta Spice Mix
- ¾ cup (72 g) Pitta Spice Mix
- ⅛ cup oz (24 g) coconut sugar
- ½ tsp (2.4 g) salt

PREPARATION

1. Weigh out all the ingredients and mix thoroughly.

Kapha
Honey Spread

🕐 5 minutes   🍴 Serves 1¾ Cup

STEP 1

1. 1¼ cup (408 g) unheated honey
2. ½ cup (72 g) Kapha Spice Mix
3. ½ tsp (2.4 g) salt

PREPARATION

1. Mix all the ingredients thoroughly.

2
Soups

Vata/Pitta/Kapha

Vegetable Soup for Everyone

🕐 20 minutes 🍴 Serves 3

STEP 1

For Vata & Pitta:

- 1½ cups (195 g) sweet potato, coarsely grated

For Kapha:

- 1½ cups (120 g) eggplant, peeled & grated

For Vata, Pitta & Kapha:

- 1½ cups (180 g) carrots, grated
- 2 cups (240 g) zucchini, grated

STEP 2

- 1 Tbsp (15 g) ghee
- 1 tsp (4 g) salt – or to taste

For Vata:

- 3 Tbsp (21 g) Vata Spice Mix
- 1 tsp (5 g) lemon juice – or to taste

For Pitta:

- 3 Tbsp (21 g) Pitta Spice Mix
- 1 tsp (5 g) lime juice – or to taste

For Kapha:

- 2 Tbsp (14 g) Hot Kapha Seed Mix
- 1 tsp (2.5 g) Hot Kapha Spice Mix
- 1 tsp (5 g) lime juice – or to taste

PREPARATION

1. Add the vegetables that suit you to a pot with 1½ half cups of water. Cook over high to medium heat for 7 to 10 minutes, until the vegetables are fully cooked. At this point the water level should be about 1 cup, if needed drain some water off. Then set aside.

2. Melt the ghee in a frying pan on a high heat. Then, turn the heat down to medium and add the suitable Spice Mix or Seed and Spice Mixes and either lemon or lime juice for Vata, Pitta or Kapha and the salt. Stir the spices continuously while the pan is getting hotter. After about 2 minutes turn off the heat and add ¼ cup of hot water. This will enrich the spices and improve the flavor.
3. Mix the spices in with the vegetables and blend to a very smooth soup, in a food processor that can support hot food.

Vata/Pitta

Black Bean, Asparagus, Avocado, Quinoa & Sweet Potato Soup

🕐 20 minutes   🍴 Serves 2

STEP 1
- 7½ Tbsp (75 g) quinoa

STEP 2
- 3 cups (350 g) asparagus, chopped
- 2 cups (150 g) sweet potato, chopped
- ⅓ (60 g) black beans - pre-cooked
- ½ cup (60 g) avocado, thinly chopped

STEP 3
- ⅓ cup (20 g) cilantro, chopped
- 1 Tbsp (15 g) ghee
- ½ tsp (3 g) salt – or to taste

For Pitta:

- 3 Tbsp (20 g) Pitta Spice Mix
- ½ tsp lime juice - or to taste

For Vata:

- 3 Tbsp (20 g) Vata Spice Mix
- ½ tsp lemon juice - or to taste

PREPARATION

1. Add the quinoa to a pot with 4 oz of water and bring rapidly to a boil, then reduce to a simmer until cooked (about 10 minutes). Take off the heat and set aside.
2. Place the asparagus and the sweet potatoes in a pot with about 3 cups of water and bring to a boil, then simmer for about 7-10 minutes. When cooked, add the pre-strained cooked black beans to vegetables.
3. Place the cilantro in a frying pan with a little water and fry on a medium heat until the water evaporates. In another pan, melt the ghee on low heat, then add the salt and the Pitta or Vata Spice Mix, and slowly stir for about 3-4 minutes to bring out the flavor. Take the pan off the heat and add the avocados to the spices and stir.
4. Put half of the cilantro and half (or all) the soup in a blender and mix thoroughly. Add the remaining cilantro in the blended soup when serving.

Vata

Asparagus and Quinoa Soup

🕐 15 minutes   🍴 Serves 2

STEP 1

- 3 Tbsp (30 g) quinoa
- 1½ cups (175 g) asparagus, chopped
- 1 cup (120 g) eggplant (aubergine), chopped
- ¾ cup (85 g) carrots, chopped

STEP 2

- ⅓ cup (15 g) fresh cilantro, chopped
- 4 Tbsp (30 g) Vata Spice Mix
- 4 tsp (20 g) ghee
- ⅝ tsp (2.5 g) salt – or to taste
- 1 tsp (4 g) lemon juice – or to taste

PREPARATION

1. Add the quinoa to a pot with 3 cups of water and bring to a boil then reduce heat to simmer.
2. After five minutes, add 2 cups of hot water and the vegetables listed in Step 1. Cook on low heat for 7 to 10 minutes until the vegetables are tender.
3. Place the cilantro in a frying pan and a ¼ cup of water and cook for about 2-3 minutes until almost all the water has evaporated.
4. Combine the cilantro with the other ingredients in step 2 and mix thoroughly. Then add the mixture to the vegetables and quinoa and stir.

   The soup is now ready to serve and goes very well with toast spread with ghee, which aids digestion.

Vata/Pitta

Carrot & Cilantro Soup

🕐 15 minutes 🍴 Serves 2

STEP 1

- 4 cups (574 g) carrots, chopped-

STEP 2

- ½ cup (60 g) cilantro, chopped
- 2 Tbsp (30 g) ghee

STEP 3

- ¾ tsp (3 g) salt, or to taste

For Pitta:

- 3 Tbsp (22 g) Pitta Spice Mix
- ¾ tsp (3.5 g) lime juice – or to taste

For Vata:

- 3 Tbsp (22 g) Vata Spice Mix
- ¾ tsp (3.5 g) lemon juice – or to taste

PREPARATION

1. Add the chopped carrots to a medium sized pot with 3 cups of water and bring to a boil, then reduce to medium heat for 7-10 minutes until the carrots are tender. Keep 3 ½ cups of water and drain off the rest.
2. Fry the cilantro in a pan with ¼ cup of water over medium heat for 2-3 minutes until the water has evaporated then set aside.
3. In a separate pan, add the ghee and lime or lemon juice, the Vata or Pitta Spice Mix and fry over low heat for 3-4 minutes to release the flavors. Then, add the carrots, half of the cooked cilantro, and a ½ cup of water from the cooked carrots. Salt to taste.
4. Put the mixture in a blender or food processor with 3 cups of water from the cooked carrots and blend until very smooth. Before serving, add the remaining half of the cilantro to give the soup some texture and color.

Vata/Pitta

Black Bean, Quinoa & Vegetables Soup

🕐 20 minutes 🍴 Serves 2

STEP 1

- ½ cup (75 g) quinoa-

STEP 2

- 3 cups (350 g) asparagus, chopped
- 2 cups (150 g) sweet potato, chopped
- ⅓ (60 g) black beans - pre-cooked
- ½ cup (60 g) avocado, thinly sliced

STEP 3

- ⅓ cup (20 g) cilantro, chopped
- 1 Tbsp (15 g) ghee
- ½ tsp (3 g) salt – or to taste

For Pitta:

- 3 Tbsp (20 g) Pitta Spice Mix
- ½ tsp (5 g) lime juice – or to taste

For Vata:

- 3 Tbsp (20 g) Vata Spice Mix
- ½ tsp (5 g) lemon juice – or to taste

PREPARATION

1. Add the quinoa to a pot with 4 oz of water and bring rapidly to a boil, then simmer until cooked (about 10 minutes). Take off the heat and set aside.
2. Place the asparagus and the sweet potatoes in a pot with about 3 cups of water and bring to a boil, then simmer for about 7-10 minutes. When cooked, add the pre-strained black beans and quinoa to the vegetable soup.
3. Place the cilantro in a frying pan with a little water and fry over medium heat until the water evaporates and add to the soup.
4. Melt the ghee on low heat, then add the salt and the Pitta or Vata Spice Mix, and slowly stir for about 3-4 minutes to bring out the flavor. Take the pan off the heat and add the avocados and lemon or lime juice to the spices and stir. Add this mixture to the soup.

5. Pour half the soup in a blender and mix until smooth then add it to the other half of the soup and stir.

Vata/Pitta

Vegetable Soup with French Lentils & Quinoa

🕐 25 minutes   🍴 Serves 3

STEP 1

- ½ cup (75 g) quinoa
- ¼ cup (60 g) French lentils

STEP 2

- 3 cups (290 g) asparagus, chopped with the ends removed
- 1¼ cup (150 g) sweet potatoes, peeled and chopped
- ⅓ cup (15 g) cilantro
- 2 cups (60 g) broccoli, chopped

STEP 3

- ½ oz (15 g) ghee
- ¾ tsp (3 g) salt – or to taste

For Vata:

- ½ tsp (5 g) lemon juice – or to taste
- 2 Tbsp (15 g) Vata Spice Mix or use half the Vata Spice Mix and add ¼ oz of Italian seasoning or Herb Mix 1.-

For Pitta:

- 1 tsp (5 g) lime juice – or to taste
- ¼ cup (30 g) coconut milk
- 2 Tbsp (15 g) Pitta Spice Mix

PREPARATION

1. Put the rinsed quinoa into a pot with 1 cup of water and stir. Place the lid on and bring to a boil over high heat, then reduce to a low heat for about 11 minutes, until fully cooked.

   Rinse the French lentils, then put them into a pot with 3 cups of water. Bring the water to a boil over high heat, then lower the heat to medium. Cook for around 15 - 20 minutes. When fully cooked, set aside.

2. Add the vegetables to a pot with 1 ½ cups of water and bring to a boil, then reduce the heat and simmer with the lid on, for 7-10 minutes.

   Add the chopped cilantro to a skillet with a ¼ cup of water and fry over medium heat for 2-3 minutes, until the cilantro is cooked. If any water has not evaporated, drain it off. Then set aside.

3. In a frying pan, melt the ghee over high heat, then reduce to medium heat.

   For the Pitta recipe, add Pitta Spice Mix, lime juice, salt and coconut milk and stir thoroughly.

   For the Vata recipe, add the Vata Spice Mix and lemon juice.

   Keep stirring for about 1 to 2 minutes then add to the vegetables and mix thoroughly.

4. Combine together the mixture with the quinoa, French lentils, vegetables and cilantro, Then place about half the soup in a blender and finely blend, then mix with the unblended soup. Keep warm until served.

Vata/Pitta

Cauliflower – Kale Soup

🕐 20 minutes 🍴 Serves 2

STEP 1

- 2 cups (160 g) carrots, sliced
- 2 cups (200 g) cauliflower, in small pieces
- 2 cup (60 g) curly kale, finely chopped
- 1 cup (60 g) celery, thinly sliced

STEP 2

- 1 oz (30 g) cilantro, chopped
- 1⅓ Tbsp (20 g) ghee
- ¾ tsp (3 g) salt – or to taste

For Pitta:

- 3 Tbsp (20 g) Pitta Spice Mix
- 1 tsp (4 g) lime juice – or to taste

For Vata:

- 3 Tbsp (20 g) Vata Spice Mix
- 1 tsp (4 g) lemon juice – or to taste

PREPARATION

1. Place all the vegetables in a pot with about 3 cups of water and bring to a boil, then simmer for about 7-10 minutes.
2. Cook the cilantro in a pan with ¼ cup of water over medium heat until the water evaporates, then set aside.
3. In another pan, heat up the ghee, lime or lemon juice and the salt. Then, add the Pitta or Vata Spice Mix and stir for about 2-3 minutes to bring out the flavor. Add to the vegetable soup with the cooked cilantro.
4. In a blender, put half of the soup and blend to a smooth texture. Then add it to the other half of the soup. Now the dish is ready to serve.

Kapha

Stew with Black Bean & Kale

⏲ 25 minutes 🍴 Serves 2

STEP 1

- 3 cups (180 g) kale, finely chopped
- 3 cups (160 g) eggplant, grated
- 3 cup (60 g) celery, finely chopped

STEP 2

- 1 Tbsp (15 g) sunflower oil
- 1 tsp (4 g) salt – or to taste
- ⅔ cup (30 g) chopped cilantro
- 2 Tbsp (16 g) Hot Kapha Seed Mix
- 2 tsp (5 g) Hot Kapha Spice Mix - or to taste
- 1 tsp (5 g) lime juice – or to taste

STEP 3

- 1 cup (120 g) cooked black beans

PREPARATION

1. Add vegetables in step one to a wok or large pan and dry fry them stirring continuously to reduce the moisture. After about 5 minutes of steaming the vegetables, set aside.
2. Add the chopped cilantro to a pan with about 1 ¼ cups of water and bring to a boil. After most of the water has boiled off, add all the ingredients in step 2 and stir.
3. Add all the ingredients in steps 1, 2 and 3 in a large pan over medium heat and mix thoroughly. This dish can be served with rice or spaghetti.

3
Wraps & Burgers

Vata

Tuna and Tahini Wrap

🕐 20 minutes　🍴 Serves 3-4

These quick and easy wraps are a rich mix of flavors. The filling can be eaten separately but ideally inside a whole wheat or gluten-free wrap, as part of a meal. Use vegetables according to the season or individual needs. For Vata types, alternative vegetables include eggplant (aubergine), cauliflower and sweet potato.

STEP 1

- 1 cup (120 g) asparagus, finely chopped with the rough ends cut off
- 1½ cup (180 g) course grated zucchini
- 1 cup (120 g) course grated carrot

STEP 2

- ¼ cup (15 g) cilantro, finely chopped
- 3 Tbsp (21 g) Vata Spice Mix
- 1½ Tbsp (22 g) ghee
- ¾ tsp (3 g) salt – or to taste
- 2 tsp (7 g) lemon juice – or to taste

STEP 3

- 4-6 ideally 6-inch or 7-inch wraps

STEP 4

- ¼ cup (60 g) tahini
- ½ cup (100 g) tuna, cooked

PREPARATION

1. Boil the asparagus in a little water for about three minutes and then add the carrots and zucchinis and cook until tender. Then take off the heat. Use only enough water to cook the vegetables so that there is no water remaining in the pan.
2. Add a little water to the cilantro and cook in a pan for about 3-4 minutes until the water has evaporated. Then add the other ingredients in step 2 and fry for another 3 minutes stirring continuously.
3. Place the wraps on a tray in the oven at 350F (175C) for about 4 minutes until hot. The wrap must remain flexible enough to fold around vegetables which means they must not be in the oven for too long. Take out of the oven and set aside. Spread a little ghee on each warm wrap (optional).

4. Place the vegetables in a pan and add all the ingredients in step 2 plus the tahini and tuna. Mix thoroughly and warm up for about 2-3 minutes.
5. Place the wrap on a tray and add about ⅓ to ½ cup (70 to 120 g) of the wrap mix in the middle, then fold it over so that it closes completely.

Pitta

Pitta Wrap with Vegetables & Avocado

🕐 20 minutes 🍴 Serves 3

STEP 1

- 1 cup (120 g) asparagus, about 10 stalks, with ends removed & finely chopped
- 1½ cups (75 g) zucchini, grated
- ½ cup (60 g) carrots, grated

STEP 2

- ½ cup (60 g) avocado, chopped finely
- ¼ cup (30 g) coconut milk
- ⅓ cup (15 g) cilantro, finely chopped
- ⅓ tsp (1.7 g) salt – or to taste
- 1 Tbsp (15 g) ghee
- 2 tsp (10 g) lime juice – or to taste
- 2½ Tbsp (15 g) Pitta Spice Mix

STEP 3

- 3 7-inch coconut flour wraps, or alternative
- 1 tbsp (15 g) ghee

PREPARATION

1. Boil the asparagus in ¼ cup of water until tender. After about three minutes, add the grated vegetables, which cook more quickly. When the water has boiled off, the vegetables should be fully cooked. Set aside.
2. Cook the cilantro in a frying pan with a little water. After the cilantro has cooked, add the avocado, the vegetables and all the other ingredients of step 2 to the frying pan and stir.
3. Preheat the oven to 350°F (180°C). Arrange the wraps on a baking sheet and spread a little ghee on each wrap. Place them in the oven for three minutes. This warms up the wraps just enough so that they are still supple enough to fold around the vegetables easily. If they bake any longer, the wraps will usually crack when you try to fold them.
4. When warm, place each wrap on a plate and arrange the vegetables in the middle of each wrap. Then fold the sides of each wrap over the filling to enclose it. These wraps could be served on their own or as an accompaniment to a soup.

Kapha

Hot Wrap with Red Pepper & Mustard Seed

🕐 20 minutes 🍴 Serves 2

STEP 1

- 1 cup (60 g) red pepper, grated
- 1 cup (30 g) broccoli, chopped
- 1 cup (120 g) asparagus, chopped
- 1¼ cups (180 g) zucchini, grated

STEP 2

- ⅓ cup (15 g) cilantro, chopped

STEP 3

- 2 tsp (5 g) Hot Kapha Spice Mix
- 1 Tbsp (8 g) Hot Kapha Seed Mix
- 1 tsp (4 g) lime juice – or to taste
- 1 Tbsp (15 g) ghee
- ½ tsp (2 g) salt – or to taste

STEP 4

- 4 about 7-inch wraps
- 1 Tbsp (15 g) sunflower oil

PREPARATION

1. Set the oven to 350 F (180 º C).
   Dry stir-fry the red peppers, broccoli, and asparagus for about 4-5 minutes then add the grated zucchini, which cooks more quickly, and stir-fry until the vegetables are well cooked. Then set aside.
2. Place the cilantro in a frying pan with ¼ cup of water and cook for about 2-3 minutes until almost all the water has evaporated.
3. Add the ghee to a frying pan on a medium to high heat. When the ghee has melted add the Hot Kapha Spice and Hot Kapha Seed Mixes and stir thoroughly for about a minute to release the flavors. Then turn the heat down and the salt and the lime juice to the frying pan and continue to stir.
4. Add the fried spices and seeds to the vegetables and the cilantro and mix thoroughly.

5. Spread the wraps with sunflower oil and place in the oven for 3 minutes to warm, but not go crispy. Then lay a wrap on a plate and place ¾ of a cup of the mix in the middle of the wrap, then fold each side over to completely cover the vegetables.

Vata

Veggie Burger

🕐 25 minutes   🍴 Serves 2-3

STEP 1

- ⅓ cup (60 g) quinoa
- 1 cup (120 g) broccoli
- 1½ cup (165 g) sweet potato
- ½ cup (60 g) carrots
- ½ cup (60 g) quick oats
- ½ cup (60 g) rice flour

STEP 2

- 1 Tbsp (15 g) Vata Spice Mix
- 1 Tbsp (8 g) Italian seasoning or Herb Mix 1 (basil, oregano & thyme)
- ¼ cup (25 g) fresh grated ginger
- 1 Tbsp (15 g) ghee
- 1 Tbsp (15 g) lemon juice – or to taste
- 1 tsp (3.5 g) salt – or to taste
- ¼ cup (60 g) breadcrumbs

STEP 3

- ¼ cup (30 g) rice flour
- 2 Tbsp (15 g) sunflower oil or ghee

PREPARATION

1. Boil the quinoa in water on a medium heat for about 10 minutes until fully cooked. Then set aside. Steam all the vegetables for about 5 minutes then mix them with the quick oats and rice flour in step 1.
2. Warm the ghee in a frying pan and add all the ingredients of Step 2 except the salt, stirring continuously to bring out the flavor. Then add that mixture with the quinoa, breadcrumbs, and the salt to the vegetables and mix thoroughly into a burger mix.
3. Take ⅓ cup of the burger mix and roll it into a ball, cover it with rice flour and press it down into a burger shape.
4. Place the sunflower oil or ghee in a skillet and fry the burger on medium heat. Use a spatula to turn it over after about 3-4 minutes.

Pitta

Veggie Burger

🕐 25 minutes 🍴 Serves 2-3

STEP 1

- ⅓ cup (60 g) quinoa
- 1 cup (120 g) broccoli, chopped
- 1¼ cup (165 g) sweet potato, grated
- ½ cup (60 g) asparagus, chopped
- ½ cup (60 g) quick oats
- ½ cup (60 g) rice flour

STEP 2

- 2 Tbsp (15 g) Pitta Spice Mix
- 1 Tbsp (8 g) rosemary & oregano
- ¼ cup (15 g) fresh grated ginger
- ½ cup (60 g) breadcrumbs
- 1 Tbsp (15 g) ghee
- 1 Tbsp (15 g) lime juice – or to taste
- 1 tsp (4 g) salt – or to taste

STEP 3

- ¼ cup (30 g) rice flour
- 2 Tbsp (15 g) sunflower oil or ghee

PREPARATION

1. Boil the quinoa in 1 ½ cups of water on a medium heat for about 10 minutes until fully cooked. Then set aside. Steam all the vegetables for about 5 minutes then mix them with the quick oats and rice flour.
2. Warm the ghee in a frying pan and add all the ingredients of Step except the salt, stirring continuously to bring out the flavor for about 2 minutes. Then add that mixture, the quinoa, the breadcrumbs, and the salt to the vegetables and mix thoroughly into a burger mix.
3. Take ⅓ cup of the burger mix and roll it into a ball, cover it with rice flour and press it down into a burger shape.
4. Place the sunflower oil or ghee in a skillet and fry the burger on medium heat. Use a spatula to turn it over after about 3-4 minutes.

Kapha

Spicy Veggie Burger

🕐 25 minutes   🍴 Serves 2-3

STEP 1

- 1 ½ cup (120 g) eggplant, peeled and grated
- 1 cup (20 g) celery, chopped
- 4 tbsp (40 g) quinoa
- ¾ cup (90 g) asparagus, chopped
- ½ cup (60 g) quick oats
- ½ cup (60 g) millet flour

STEP 2

- 2 tbsp (15 g) Kapha Spice Mix
- ⅛ cup (5 g) basil
- ½ cup (30 g) fresh ginger
- ½ cup (60 g) breadcrumbs
- 1 Tbsp (15 g) ghee
- 1 Tbsp (15 g) lime juice – or to taste
- ¾ tsp (3 g) salt – or to taste

STEP 3

- ¼ cup (30 g) millet flour or buckwheat flour
- 2 Tbsp (30 g) sunflower oil or ghee

PREPARATION

1. Boil the quinoa in water on a medium heat for about 10 minutes until fully cooked, then set aside. Dry stir-fry the eggplant for about 3 minutes then add all the other vegetables to fry for about 5-7 minutes until fully cooked. Stir continuously. Once cooked, mix in the quick oats, the breadcrumbs and millet flour.
2. Warm the ghee in a frying pan and add all the ingredients of Step 2, stirring continuously to bring out the flavor. Then add that mixture and the quinoa to the vegetables and mix thoroughly into a burger mix.
3. Take ⅓ cup of the burger mix and roll it into a ball, cover it with millet flour and press it down into a burger shape.
4. Place the sunflower oil or ghee in a skillet and fry the burger on medium heat. Use a spatula to turn it over after about 2-4 minutes.

4
Omelets

Vata/Pitta

Omelet with Asparagus & Avocado

🕐 15 minutes 🍴 Serves 2

STEP 1

- ½ cup (60 g) asparagus, chopped & ends removed
- ½ cup (60 g) carrot, grated
- ½ cup (45 g) zucchini, grated

STEP 2

- ½ (60 g) avocado, chopped

For Vata:

- 1 Tbsp (7 g) Vata Spice Mix

For Pitta:

- 1 Tbsp (7 g) Pitta Spice Mix
- 1 Tbsp (15 g) ghee
- ½ tsp (2 g) salt – or to taste

STEP 3

For Vata:

- 1½ Tbsp (4 g) dried basil or Italian Seasoning

For Pitta:

- 1 ½ Tbsp (4 g) dried rosemary or basil-3 eggs (160 g)
- ⅜ tsp (1.5 g) salt – or to taste
- 1 Tbsp (15 g) ghee

PREPARATION

1. Place all the vegetables in Step 1 in a pot filled with ½ cup of water, bring to a boil over high heat, then reduce to medium heat. Cook for 4 to 5 minutes. Drain off all the water, then set aside.
2. Melt the ghee in a frying pan over high heat, then add the Spice Mix, salt and chopped avocado and stir continuously for about a minute or two. Then mix in all the vegetables in Step 1 and set aside.

3. In a mixing bowl, beat the eggs and add the salt, herbs of Step 3. Mix all together, then set aside.

   Melt ⅔ Tbsp of ghee in a frying pan, over high heat. When the ghee is quite hot, pour the egg mixture into the frying pan and ensure it fills the pan.

   Cook the eggs for 2-3 minutes. Then add the spices and the vegetables to one half of the omelet only and fold over the other half to seal in all the vegetables. Reduce the heat to medium - low for about 2 minutes. The omelet is now ready to serve.

Kapha

Omelet with Asparagus & Eggplant

🕒 15 minutes   🍴 Serves 1-2

STEP 1

- ½ cup (60 g) asparagus, chopped
- ½ cup (60 g) eggplant, grated
- ½ cup (45 g) zucchini, grated

STEP 2

- 2 Tbsp (16 g) Hot Kapha Seed and Spice Mix
- 1 tsp (5 g) Hot Kapha Spice Mix – or to taste
- 1 Tbsp (10 g) ghee or sunflower oil
- ⅜ tsp (1.5 g) salt – or to taste

STEP 3

- 1½ Tbsp (4 g) dried basil or Italian Seasoning
- 3 eggs (160 g)
- ⅜ tsp (1.5 g) salt – or to taste
- ⅔ Tbsp (10 g) ghee

PREPARATION

1. Dry stir-fry all the vegetables in Step 1, ideally in a wok or a frying pan. Stir for about 4-5 minutes over medium heat to reduce the moisture content. When fully cooked, set aside.
2. Melt 1 tbsp of ghee to a frying pan over high heat, add the Hot Kapha Spice Mix and the salt and stir continuously for about a minute or two. Then, add the mixture to the vegetables and stir.
3. Beat the eggs and add the salt, basil, or Italian seasoning, in a mixing bowl, and set aside.
4. Melt ⅔ Tbsp of ghee in an 8 x 10 frying pan over high heat. When the ghee is quite hot pour the egg mixture into the frying pan and ensure it fills up the whole pan. After 2-3 minutes, add the vegetables on one side of the omelette only. Then fold over the other half to seal in all the vegetables. Then turn to a medium to low heat for about 2 minutes. The omelet is now ready to serve.

5

Paneer Dishes

Vata/Pitta/Kapha

How to Make Paneer

🕒 15 minutes

STEP 1

- 4 cups (1 L) milk
- ⅛ cup (30 g) fresh or bottled lemon or lime juice, or yoghurt.

PREPARATION

1. Bring the milk slowly to a boil in a deep pot. Just before the boiling point, add the lemon or lime juice or yogurt and mix it around slowly. The milk will start to curdle into small clumps.
2. Simply drain off the yellow liquid (whey). You can drink the whey or store it for other uses. Whey has good nutritional value.

   The amount of curd will be about ⅙ of the milk used to make the paneer. Paneer is used in several recipes.

Vata

Paneer with Baby Spinach & Asparagus

🕐 15 minutes   🍴 Serves 2-3

STEP 1

- 1 ⅓ cups (200 g) paneer, small chunks
- 1 cup (60 g) baby spinach, chopped finely
- ¾ cup (75 g) 6-7 asparagus, chopped finely

STEP 2

- 1 Tbsp (15 g) ghee
- 1 tsp (5 g) lemon juice – or to taste
- 2 Tbsp (15 g) cumin seeds
- 2 Tbsp (14 g) Vata Spice Mix
- ½ tsp (2 g) salt – or to taste
- 1 Tbsp (6 g) fresh ginger, optional

PREPARATION

1. Steam the asparagus and baby spinach until tender. Set aside.
2. Melt the ghee in a frying pan and add all the other ingredients in step 2. Stir-fry for about 2-3 minutes. Then, add the paneer and the vegetables and stir gently for 1-2 more minutes on low heat.

Vata

Avocado and Peas with Paneer

🕐 5 minutes   🍴 Serves 3

STEP 1

- ¾ cup (150 g) paneer, small chunks
- ½ cup (60 g) peas (frozen)
- ½ cup (60 g) ripe avocado (mashed)

STEP 2

- ⅓ cup (20 g) cilantro, chopped
- 1 Tbsp (15 g) ghee
- 1 tsp (5 g) lemon juice – or to taste
- 2 Tbsp (14 g) Vata Spice Mix
- 1 Tbsp (15 g) cumin seeds
- 1 Tbsp (15 g) mustard seeds
- ½ tsp (1.5 g) salt – or to taste
- optional: ⅓ cup (30 g) fresh grated ginger

PREPARATION

1. Boil the cilantro in a little water for about 3-4 minutes until fully cooked. Set aside.
2. Boil the frozen peas in a little water until they are fully cooked, then set aside.
3. Heat the ghee in a frying pan, then add the cumin and mustard seeds and grated ginger. Fry until the seeds start popping. Reduce the heat to low and add the other ingredients of Steps 1 & 2. Stir gently for 2 minutes.

   The dish should have somebody to it. It would go well with kitchari or rice & vegetables or salmon.

Pitta

Paneer with Baby Spinach & Asparagus

⏱ 15 minutes   🍴 Serves 2-3

STEP 1

- 1⅓ cup (200 g) paneer
- 1 cup (60 g) baby spinach, chopped finely
- ½ cup (75 g) 6-7 asparagus, chopped finely

STEP 2

- 1 Tbsp (15 g) ghee
- 1 tsp (5 g) lime juice – or to taste
- ⅓ cup (70 g) coconut milk
- 2 Tbsp (14 g) Pitta Spice Mix
- ½ tsp (2 g) salt – or to taste

PREPARATION

1. Boil the asparagus in 1 cup of water for about 5-7 minutes, until tender. In a separate pan, place the baby spinach in about ½ cup of water and cook for about 4 minutes over medium-high heat, until tender. Take off the heat. Then drain off all the water in both pans and set aside.
2. Melt the ghee in a frying pan and add all the other ingredients in step 2. Stir while frying for about 2-3 minutes. Then, add the paneer and the vegetables and stir gently for 1-2 minutes on low heat. The dish is now ready to add to the main meal.

Pitta

Paneer with Asparagus & Tahini

🕐 15 minutes   🍴 Serves 2

STEP 1

- ½ cup (60 g) asparagus, chopped

STEP 2

- 1 Tbsp (15 g) ghee
- ⅓ cup (20 g) cilantro, chopped

STEP 3

- ½ cup (60 g) half an avocado, mashed
- 1⅓ cup (200 g) paneer, diced
- 1 tsp (5 g) lime juice – or to taste
- 2 Tbsp (30 g) coconut milk
- 2 Tbsp (30 g) cumin seeds – optional
- ½ tsp (2 g) salt, or to taste
- 2 Tbsp (40 g) tahini
- 2 Tbsp (30 g) Pitta Spice Mix – or to taste

PREPARATION

1. Boil the asparagus in one cup of water for about five minutes until tender and set aside.
2. Melt the ghee in a frying pan, add about ¼ cup of water with the chopped cilantro, then cook until almost all the water boils off. Then lower the heat to simmer.
3. Add all the remaining ingredients in step 3 to the frying pan and mix thoroughly.

   The dish is now ready to serve and will go well with almost all other main course dishes.

Pitta

Paneer with Peas, Avocado & Tahini

🕐 15 minutes 🍴 Serves 3

STEP 1

- ¾ cup (120 g) peas

STEP 2

- 1 cup (180 g) paneer, small chunks
- ¾ cup (90 g) avocado, mashed
- ⅓ cup (20 g) cilantro, chopped
- 2 Tbsp (30 g) ghee
- 2 tsp (10 g) lime juice – or to taste
- 4 Tbsp (30 g) Pitta Spice Mix
- 1 tsp (3 g) salt or to taste
- ⅙ cup (30 g) coconut milk
- 2 Tbsp (30 g) mustard seeds – or to taste

2 oz (60g) tahini

PREPARATION

1. Boil the peas until cooked then set aside.
2. Boil the cilantro in a frying pan with ¼ cup of water, until they are fully cooked, then set aside.
Heat up half the ghee to a frying pan and add the mustard seeds, stirring until they pop, then take off the heat.
In a separate pan, heat up the rest of the ghee before adding the Pitta Spice Mix, the salt and the coconut milk and fry for 1 - 3 minutes. Then, add all the other ingredients and stir gently for 1-2 more minutes over low heat. The dish is now ready to serve and would go well in a warm wrap.

Kapha

Paneer with Baby Spinach & Asparagus

15 minutes Serves 2-3

STEP 1

- 1⅓ cup (200 g) paneer small chunks
- 1 cup (60 g) baby spinach, chopped finely
- ¾ cup (75 g) 6-7 asparagus, chopped finely

STEP 2

- 1 Tbsp (15 g) ghee
- 1 tsp (5 g) lime juice – or to taste
- 1 Tbsp (8 g) Hot Kapha Seed Mix
- 1 tsp (2.5 g) Hot Kapha Spice Mix
- ½ tsp (2 g) salt – or to taste

PREPARATION

1. Boil the asparagus in 1 cup of water for about 5-7 minutes, until tender. Cook the baby spinach in about ½ cup of water in a separate pan on medium-high heat. After about 4 minutes, take off the heat when tender. Then drain off all the water in both pans and set aside.
2. Melt the ghee in a frying pan and add all the other ingredients in step 2. Stir while frying for about 2-3 minutes. Then, add the paneer and the vegetables and stir gently on low heat for 1-2 more minutes. The dish is now ready to add to your meal.

Kapha

Paneer with Eggplant, Asparagus and Hot Kapha Spice & Seed Mix

🕐 15 minutes   🍴 Serves 3

STEP 1

- 1 cup (150 g) paneer, cubed
- ½ cup (60 g) asparagus, chopped
- ½ cup (60 g) eggplant (aubergine), chopped into small pieces.

STEP 2

- ⅓ cup (30 g) cilantro, chopped
- 1 Tbsp (15 g) ghee
- 1 tsp (5 g) lime juice – or to taste
- 2 Tbsp (16 g) Hot Kapha Seed Mix
- 1 tsp (2.5 g) Hot Kapha Spice Mix
- ½ tsp (1.5 g) salt – or to taste
- ¼ cup (15 g) fresh ginger

PREPARATION

1. Boil the asparagus in 1 cup of water for about 4-5 minutes until tender then set aside. Cook the eggplant in a separate pan with ½ a cup of water, for about 5 minutes, until tender. Boil the cilantro in ¼ cup of water for about 3 minutes, until fully cooked. Grate the ginger and set aside
2. In a separate frying pan, melt the ghee over medium heat, then add the Hot Kapha spice mix and sauté for about 1-2 minutes to bring out the flavor. Then add all the ingredients of Steps 1 & 2 together with salt to taste and stir gently for another minute or two.

The dish would go well with kitchari, rice & spicy vegetables, or fish such as mackerel or salmon.

Kapha

Paneer with Baby Spinach & Asparagus

🕒 15 minutes 🍴 Serves 2-3

STEP 1

- 1⅓ cup (200 g) paneer, small chunks
- 1 cup (60 g) baby spinach, chopped finely
- ¾ cup (75 g) 6-7 asparagus, chopped finely

STEP 2

- 1 Tbsp (15 g) ghee
- 1 tsp (5 g) lime juice – or to taste
- 2 Tbsp (16 g) Hot Kapha Seed Mix
- 2 tsp (5 g) Hot Kapha Spice Mix - or to taste
- ½ tsp (2 g) salt – or to taste

PREPARATION

1. Boil the asparagus in 1 cup of water for about 5-7 minutes until tender. Cook the baby spinach in about ½ cup of water in a separate pan over medium-high heat. After 4 minutes, test if tender then take off the heat. Drain off all the water in both pans and set aside.
2. Melt the ghee in a frying pan and add all the other ingredients in step 2. Stir while frying for about 2-3 minutes. Then add the paneer and vegetables and stir gently for 1-2 more minutes over low heat. The dish is now ready to add to the main meal.

6

Main Meals

Vata

Mung Beans with Vegetables

⏲ 20 minutes   🍴 Serves 3

STEP 1

- ½ cup (100 g) mung bean, rinsed
- 1 cube of bouillon (10 g), or ½ Tbsp of powdered bouillon

STEP 2

- 1 cup (120 g) asparagus, about 12 stalks, finely chopped
- 1 cup (130 g) sweet potato, cubed
- 1 cup (100 g) zucchini, chopped
- 1 cup (120 g) carrots, chopped

STEP 3

- ⅓ cup (15 g) cilantro, finely chopped
- salt to taste
- 1 Tbsp (15 g) ghee
- 2 tsp (8 g) lemon juice
- 2 Tbsp (15 g) Vata Spice Mix

PREPARATION

1. In a medium size pot, add 3 cups of water and the mung beans. Cook over a medium heat for 15 minutes then add the bouillon and cook for a further 5 minutes, until tender. Drain off to leave ½ cup of the water and set aside.
2. Pour 2 cups of water in a pot and add the vegetables, except the asparagus. Cook for about 10 minutes, until tender. Keep ¼ cup of water from the vegetables.
3. In a frying pan, cook the chopped asparagus in ½ cup of water for about 5 minutes until tender and add to the vegetables.
4. Cook the cilantro in a frying pan with ⅓ cup of water until the evaporates.
5. Combine all the ingredients in Step 3 with the vegetables, ¼ cup of vegetable water, the mung beans with the ½ cup of water and heat up over low heat. Optionally blend one third of the vegetables for a creamy texture.

Vata

Tuna and Tahini

🕐 20 minutes 🍴 Serves 2-3

STEP 1

- 1 cup (120 g) asparagus, chopped with the rough ends cut off
- 1½ cup (180 g) zucchini, chopped
- 1 cup (120 g) carrot, chopped

STEP 2

- ¼ cup (15 g) cilantro, finely chopped
- 3 Tbsp (21 g) Vata Spice Mix
- 1½ Tbsp (22 g) ghee
- ¾ tsp (3 g) salt – or to taste
- 2 tsp (7 g) lemon juice – or to taste

STEP 3

- ¼ cup (60 g) tahini
- ½ cup (100 g) tuna, cooked

PREPARATION

1. Boil the asparagus in a little water for about 3 minutes and then add the carrots and zucchinis and cook until tender. Then take off the heat. Use only enough water to cook the vegetables so that there is no water remaining in the pan.
2. Add ¼ cup of water to the cilantro and cook in a pan for about 3-4 minutes, until the water has evaporated. Then, add the other ingredients in step 2 and fry for another 3 minutes stirring continuously.
3. Add all the ingredients in steps 2 and 3 to the vegetables and mix thoroughly while warming up for about 2-3 minutes over low heat.

Pitta

French Lentils with Vegetables

🕒 20 minutes   🍴 Serves 3

STEP 1

- ½ cup (80 g) French lentils, rinsed
- 1 cube of bouillon, or ½ Tbsp of powdered bouillon (10 g)

STEP 2

- 1 cup (120 g) asparagus, about 12 stalks, finely chopped
- 1 cup (130 g) sweet potato, cubed
- 1 cup (100 g) zucchini, chopped
- 1 cup (120 g) carrots, chopped

STEP 3

- ¼ cup (30 g) coconut milk
- ⅓ cup (15 g) cilantro, finely chopped
- salt to taste
- 1 Tbsp (15 g) ghee
- 2½ tsp (10 g) lime juice
- 1½ Tbsp (15 g) Pitta Spice Mix

PREPARATION

1. In a medium size pot, add 3½ cups of water, the French lentils and the bouillon. Cook over medium heat for about 35 minutes, until tender. Drain off the ½ cup of the water and set aside.
2. Pour 2 cups of water in a pot and add the vegetables, except the asparagus. Cook for about 10 minutes, until tender. Keep ¼ cup of water from the vegetables.
3. In a frying pan, cook the chopped asparagus in ½ cup of water for about 5 minutes until tender and add to the vegetables.
4. Cook the cilantro in a frying pan with ⅓ cup of water until the evaporates.
5. Combine all the ingredients in Step 3 with the vegetables, ¼ cup of vegetable water, the French lentils and heat up over low heat. Optionally blend one third of the vegetables for a good texture.

Pitta

Stew with French Lentils & Vegetables

⏲ 30 minutes   🍴 Serves 3

STEP 1

- 2 cup (70 g) kale, chopped
- ¾ cup (90 g) butternut squash, chopped
- 1½ cups (75 g) zucchini, chopped
- ½ cup (60 g) carrots, chopped

STEP 2

- ½ cup (80 g) French lentils
- 1 cube of bouillon, or ½ Tbsp of powdered bouillon or stock cube (10 g)

STEP 3

- ½ cup (60 g) avocado, chopped
- ¼ cup (30 g) coconut milk
- ⅓ cup (15 g) cilantro, finely chopped
- if required, add a little salt to taste
- 2 Tbsp (30 g) ghee
- 2½ tsp (10 g) lime juice – or to taste
- 2 Tbsp (15 g) Pitta Spice Mix

PREPARATION

1. Place all the vegetables in a pot with 3 cups of water and set on a medium to high heat for 10 minutes. When cooked, drain off all but ½ cup of water. Then set aside.
2. Cook the French lentils in a pot with 2 cups of water on a medium to high heat for 15 minutes. After 10 minutes, check the lentils to see if they are tender. When cooked, drain off the water and set aside.
3. Add the cilantro to a frying pan with the ghee and ¼ cup of water and cook on a medium to high heat until almost all the water has boiled off. Then add the avocado, the spices, the coconut milk, lime juice and the salt. Cook for another 1-2 minutes. Then add the vegetables and French lentils and mix thoroughly.
4. Blend one third of the vegetables until smooth, then add back to the vegetables and mix thoroughly. The dish is now ready to serve and goes very well with paneer and rice.

Pitta

Stew with Asparagus & Paneer

🕐 25 minutes 🍴 Serves 2

STEP 1

- 1 cup (120 g) asparagus, chopped after the rough ends are cut off
- 1 cup (170 g) butternut squash, chopped
- 1 cup (120 g) carrots, chopped
- 2 cups (40 g) celery, chopped

STEP 2

- 3 Tbsp (21 g) Pitta Spice Mix
- 1½ Tbsp (22 g) ghee
- ¾ tsp (3.5 g) salt – or to taste
- 2 tsp (10 g) lime juice – or to taste

STEP 3

- 1⅔ cup (250 g) paneer

PREPARATION

1. Place all the chopped vegetables in a pot with 1½ cups of water and cook on a medium heat for about 7-10 minutes until tender. Then drain the water until there is ¼ cup of water remaining.
2. Heat the ghee in a frying pan on medium heat. When fully melted, add the Pitta Spice Mix, lime juice and the salt. Stir for a little longer to bring out the flavor.
3. Add the spices and paneer to the vegetables and stir gently over low heat for 1-2 minutes.
4. Blend one third of the mixture, then add it to the remaining vegetables and serve warm.

   This dish goes well with rice and split mung dal or kitchari.

Vata/Pitta/Kapha

Pan-Fried Chicken in Ghee

🕐 10 minutes   🍴 Serves 3

STEP 1

- 1 Tbsp (15 g) ghee
- Two breasts (650 g) chicken, cut into small chunks about one inch by ½ an inch.
- ½ tsp (2 g) salt – or to taste

OPTIONAL

- ½ Tbsp (2 g) basil or rosemary

PREPARATION

1. Warm the ghee in a skillet over medium heat for about 2 minutes. Add the cut chicken and stir for about 1 minute then add the salt and the herbs.
   Reduce the heat to medium-low and place the lid over the chicken.
2. Stir about every 3 minutes until all the chicken pieces are cooked, usually in just under 10 minutes. Then take off the heat and set aside ready to serve with the rest of the meal.

Kapha

Stew with Black Bean & Kale

🕐 25 minutes 🍴 Serves 3

STEP 1

- 3 cups (180 g) kale, finely chopped
- 2 cups (160 g) eggplant, grated
- ⅓ cup (60 g) celery, finely chopped

STEP 2

- 1 Tbsp (15 g) sunflower oil
- 1 tsp (4 g) salt – or to taste
- ⅔ cup (30 g) chopped cilantro
- 2 Tbsp (16 g) Hot Kapha Seed Mix
- 2 tsp (5 g) Hot Kapha Spice Mix – or to taste
- 1 tsp (5 g) lime juice – or to taste

STEP 3

- 1 cup (120 g) cooked black beans

PREPARATION

1. Add vegetables in step one to a wok or large pan and dry fry them stirring continuously to reduce the moisture. After about 5 minutes of steaming the vegetables, set aside.
2. Add the chopped cilantro to a pan with about 1¼ cups of water and bring to a boil. After most of the water has boiled off, add all the ingredients in step 2 and stir.
3. Add all the ingredients in steps 1, 2 and 3 in a large pan over medium heat and mix thoroughly. This dish can be served with rice or spaghetti.

Kapha

Brown Lentils with Vegetables

🕐 20 minutes　🍴 Serves 3

STEP

- ½ cup (100 g) brown lentils, rinsed
- 1 cube of bouillon (10 g), or ½ Tbsp of powdered bouillon

STEP 2

- 1 cup (120 g) asparagus, about 12 stalks, finely chopped
- 1 cup (130 g) butternut squash, chopped
- 1 cup (100 g) zucchini, chopped
- 1 cup (120 g) eggplant, peeled and chopped

STEP 3

- ⅓ cup (15 g) cilantro, finely chopped
- Salt to taste
- 2 tsp (5 g) Hot Kapha Spice Mix
- 2 Tbsp (16 g) Hot Kapha Seed Mix
- 1 Tbsp (10 g) ghee
- 2 tsp (8 g) lime juice – or to taste

PREPARATION

1. In a medium size pot, add 3 cups of water and the brown lentils. Cook over a medium heat for 15 minutes, until tender. Drain off to leave ¼ cup of the water and set aside.
2. Pour 2 cups of water in a pot and add the vegetables, except the asparagus. Cook for about 8 minutes then add the bouillon and cook for a further 5 minutes, until tender, then set aside. Leave ½ cup of water with the vegetables.
3. In a frying pan, cook the chopped asparagus in ½ cup of water for about 5 minutes until tender and add to the vegetables.
4. Cook the cilantro in a frying pan with ⅓ cup of water until the water evaporates and add to the vegetables.
5. Heat the oil in a frying pan over medium-high heat. Add the Hot Kapha Spice and Seed Mixes and stir thoroughly for about 2 minutes to release the flavors. Then turn the heat down, add the salt and the lime juice and continue to stir for ½ minute.
6. Combine the spices, the lentils and ¼ cup of water from the lentils with the vegetables, and simmer until served. Optionally, blend one third of the vegetables for a creamy texture.

Kapha

Spicy Eggplant & Kale

🕐 20 minutes   🍴 Serves 2

STEP 1

- 2 cups (160 g) eggplant, peeled and chopped
- 1 cup (60 g) kale, chopped
- 1 cup (120 g) asparagus, chopped
- 1¼ cups (180 g) zucchini, grated

STEP 2

- ½ oz (15 g) cilantro, chopped

STEP 3

- 2 tsp (5 g) Hot Kapha Spice Mix
- 2 Tbsp (16 g) Hot Kapha Seed Mix
- 1 tsp (4 g) lime juice – or to taste
- 1 Tbsp (15 g) ghee
- ½ tsp (2 g) salt – or to taste

PREPARATION

1. In a large frying pan, dry stir-fry the eggplant, kale, and asparagus for about 4-5 minutes then add the grated zucchini, which cooks more quickly, and stir until the vegetables are well cooked. Set aside.
2. Place the cilantro in a frying pan with ¼ cup of water and cook for about 2-3 minutes until almost all the water has evaporated. Then, add to the vegetables and stir.
3. Melt the ghee in a frying pan over medium-high heat. Then, add the Hot Kapha Spice and Hot Kapha Seed Mixes and stir continuously for about two minutes to release the flavors. Turn down the heat and add the salt and the lime juice and stir. Combine with the vegetables and mix thoroughly.

Vata/Pitta/Kapha

Lassi

🕐 4 minutes 🍴 Serves 2-3

STEP 1

- ¾ cup (175 g) plain yogurt
- 1½ cups (375 g) water

STEP 2

- ½ tsp (2.25 g) salt, or to taste
- 3 Tbsp (10 g) cilantro, chopped

For Vata

- 1 tsp (2.5 g) cumin
- 1 tsp (2.5 g) powdered ginger

For Pitta:

- 2 tsp (5 g) fennel
- 1 tsp (2.5 g) cumin
- ½ tsp (1.2 g) powdered ginger

For Kapha:

- 1 tsp (2.5 g) cumin
- 2 Tbsp (7 g) powdered ginger

PREPARATION

1. Mix the plain yoghurt with the water in a blender for up to 45 seconds. Blending yogurt with water makes the lassi lighter and more digestible as well as enhancing the power of your digestion.
2. Add the ingredients appropriate for the type required in Step 2 and blend a second time for around 15 seconds.

Vata/Pitta/Kapha

White Basmati Rice

🕒 15 minutes 🍴 Serves 4

STEP 1

- 1 cup (180 g) white basmati rice
- 1 tsp (3 g) cumin seeds – optional
- ½ tsp (1.5 g) turmeric – optional

STEP 2

- ½ tsp (2 g) salt - or to taste

PREPARATION

1. Rinse the rice in water five times to clean it. Then add to a pan with 3 cups of water. Add the cumin seeds and turmeric and bring to the boil, then simmer with a lid on for 10 – 15 minutes until fully cooked.

2. Drain off any excess water and then add salt to taste.

Vata/Pitta/Kapha

Roast Potatoes with Ghee

🕐 75 minutes   🍴 Serves 4

This is a real treat and cooking the potatoes in ghee with rosemary gives a really rich taste with crispy potatoes.

STEP 1

- 3-4 medium sized (565 g) potatoes
- 1 Tbsp (4 g) rosemary leaf or basil - or to taste
- ¼ cup (60 g) ghee
- 1 tsp (4 g) finely ground salt – or to taste

PREPARATION

1. Peel the potatoes and cut them into sizes about 1 to 1.5 oz, (30 to 45 g). Place the ghee in a baking tray and set the oven to 375°F (195°C) . Chop the rosemary in slightly smaller pieces. Take the baking tray out when the ghee is fully melted but not very hot. Roll the potatoes in the ghee so that they are covered fully then add the rosemary leaves and the finely ground salt. Then place in the oven for 90 minutes. If you have less time than that you can boil the potatoes in water first for about 15 minutes, then take them out of the water and let then dry off before covering them in ghee and the rosemary leaves. But the potatoes are not as good and fully roasted in ghee.

2. While in the over every 30 minutes approximately turn them over and use a spoon to cover them in the same ghee they are already in. This produces the most well roasted potatoes.

3. Checking them every 30 minutes also prevents over cooking them.

Vata/Pitta/Kapha

Dhal

🕐 25 minutes   🍴 Serves 3

STEP 1

- ½ cup (120 g) mung beans, rinsed 5 times
- ⅓ cup (1.4 g) salt – or to taste

PREPARATION

1. Add the dhal and 2 ½ cups of water to a pot and place on a high heat until the water boils, then reduce to a low to moderate heat and cook for about 20 minutes. When the dal is cooked, add to a sieve to remove all the water, and set aside. If this is to be served on its own, you may want to add ⅓ tsp salt and chopped cooked cilantro.

Vata/Pitta/Kapha

Quinoa

🕐 10 minutes   🍴 Serves 2

STEP 1

- ½ cup (85 g) quinoa, washed
- 1 tsp (3 g) cumin seeds – optional
- 1 tsp (3 g) turmeric – optional

STEP 2

- ¼ tsp (1 g) salt - or to taste

PREPARATION

1. Add the quinoa to a pot with 2 ½ cups of water and place on a medium heat, add any optional spices or seeds and cook for 15 minutes. Or until cooked.
2. Drain off any excess water and add salt to taste.

Vata/Pitta/Kapha

Pan-Fried Chicken in Ghee

🕐 10 minutes   🍴 Serves 3

STEP 1

- 1 Tbsp (15 g) ghee
- Two breasts (650 g) chicken, cut into small chunks about one inch by ½ an inch.
- ½ tsp (2 g) salt – or to taste

OPTIONAL:

- ½ tsp (2 g) basil or rosemary

PREPARATION

1. Warm the ghee in a skillet over medium heat for about 2 minutes. Add the cut chicken and stir for about 1 minute then add the salt and the herbs.
2. Reduce the heat to medium-low and place the lid over the chicken.
3. Stir about every 3 minutes until all the chicken pieces are cooked, usually in just under 10 minutes. Then take off the heat and set aside ready to serve with the rest of the meal.

Vata/Pitta

Nut Roast with Walnuts

🕐 100 minutes   🍴 Serves 5

STEP 1

- 2 cup (240 g) asparagus - with the rough ends cut off and then finely chopped
- 1¾ cups (210 g) zucchini, finely chopped
- 3 cups (180 g) walnuts – soaked overnight, then broken into pieces
- ⅓ cup (60 g) quinoa or dhal
- ¼ cup (90 g) chopped butternut squash
- ¼ cup (90 g) chopped sweet potato
- ½ cup (60 g) breadcrumbs
- 1¼ cup (90 g) quick oats

STEP 2

- ⅓ cup (12 g) Italian seasoning, or Herb Mix 1 (basil, oregano & thyme), or basil
- ¼ cup (30 g) cilantro, chopped
- 1½ Tbsp (6 g) salt, or to taste
- 2 Tbsp (30 g) ghee

For Vata:

- 2 Tbsp (15 g) Vata Spice Mix
- 3 Tbsp (30 g) fresh ginger, finely grated
- 1 Tbsp (4 g) black pepper
- 1 Tbsp (15 g) lemon juice, or to taste

For Pitta:

- 2 Tbsp (15 g) Pitta Spice Mix
- 1 Tbsp (15 g) lime juice, or to taste

PREPARATION

1. Set the oven at 350ºF (180ºC)
2. Steam or boil all the vegetables for about 10 minutes until still a little firm (al dente). Combine the oats, breadcrumbs and vegetables in a bowl and add a quarter cup of water. Set aside.
3. In a pot, add 3 cups of water to the quinoa or dhal and cook for 10 minutes over medium heat. Drain when cooked.

4. Put the cilantro in a pan with ¼ cup of water and boil until the water has evaporated, then set aside.
5. Melt the ghee in a pan over medium heat. Turn down the heat to low and add all the ingredients in step 2 except the lemon juice, cilantro, and salt. Stir continuously for a few minutes. Take the pan off the heat and add the lemon juice, cilantro, and salt and mix thoroughly. The mixture should be a little firm, not runny. Some moisture will be absorbed by the uncooked oats.
6. Combine all the ingredients of Steps 1 and 2 in a large bowl and place the mixture into a 9 x 5 casserole greased with sunflower oil or ghee. Bake for 40 to 60 minutes until the nut roast is brown at the edges.

Vata/Pitta/Kapha

Kitchari

🕐 25 minutes   🍴 Serves 3

STEP 1

- ½ cups (100 g) dhal, rinsed 5 times
- ½ cups (100 g) basmati rice, rinsed 5 times
- ½ tsp (2 g) salt – or to taste

PREPARATION

1. Place both ingredients in a pan with 3 cups of water and boil on a medium heat for 15 to 20 minutes until tender. Drain off any excess water and add the salt.
2. Optionally add cumin seeds, turmeric, cooked chopped cilantro and a few finely chopped cooked vegetables.

Vata

Stew with Asparagus, Zucchini & Tahini

🕐 25 minutes 🍴 Serves 2

STEP 1

- 1 cup (120 g) asparagus, finely chopped with the rough ends cut off
- 1½ cup (180 g) zucchini, chopped
- 1 cup (120 g) carrot, chopped
- ½ cube of bouillon (5 g), or ½ Tbsp of powdered bouillon
- salt - to taste

STEP 2

- ¼ cup (15 g) cilantro, finely chopped
- 3 Tbsp (21 g) Vata Spice Mix
- 1½ Tbsp (22 g) ghee
- 2 tsp (7 g) lemon juice – or to taste

STEP 3

- ¼ cup (60 g) tahini

PREPARATION

1. Boil carrots and zucchinis with 1½ cups of water and cook until tender. Then take off the heat and drain off all the excess water.
2. Boil the asparagus in ½ a cup of water with the bouillon for about five minutes until tender, then mix with the other vegetables keeping all the water with the flavors. Then set aside.
3. Add the cilantro to ¼ a cup of water in a pan and cook for about 4-5 minutes until tender when most of the water has evaporated. Then add the other ingredients in step 2 and stir on a low heat to release the flavors from the spices.
4. Add all the ingredients including the tahini to a pot on a low heat and mix thoroughly. Then take about one third of the mix and blend to give a creamy consistency. Then mix with the remaining ingredients. The dish is now ready to serve.

7
Desserts

Vata/Pitta

Custard

🕐 10 minutes   🍴 Serves 2

STEP 1

- 3 cups milk (750 g)

STEP 2

- 1 ¾ Tbsp (27 g) coconut sugar
- ½ Tbsp (7 g) vanilla extract
- 3-4 Tbsp cornstarch (30 - 40 g)
- ½ Tbsp (7 g) cardamom
- 1 Tbsp (2.5 g) ground nutmeg
- 2 tsp (10 g) cinnamon for Vata (optional)

PREPARATION

1. Pour ⅓ cup of the milk in a cup, add all the Step 2 ingredients, and stir to combine the corn-starch fully.
2. Heat the rest of the milk in a saucepan over medium-high heat. Right before the boiling point, turn down the heat to low and add the mixed ingredients. Stir until fully thickened, about 2-3 minutes. Remove from the heat and serve.
3. This simple custard can be used in many ways, such as a complement to a pear or apple crumble.

Pitta

Rice Pudding

🕐 2 Hours 🍴 Serves 3

Rice pudding has the potential to be balancing for many people and here we offer four versions to choose from.

1. Milk with cardamom and nutmeg
2. ½ milk and ½ of half and half cream
3. With half coconut water and half coconut milk and blended dates or raisins & water
4. Oat milk

All of these versions can be sweetened with either coconut sugar, dates or raisins blended with a little water. Dates and raisins are good for both Vata and Pitta types. It is easy to try both as the date or raisin pulp can be added to the rice pudding or as a side dish to serve up for each individual.

With these different types of milk and sweeteners you will have to adjust the quantity to suit your taste. The dates and raisins need about half the amount of water to give them the right consistency.

Arborio rice is traditional for rice pudding, but basmati rice is also OK and has more protein.

STEP 1

- A little under 5 cups (1200 g) milk, or milk & half and half, or half coconut water and half coconut milk, or oat milk
- ½ cup (75 g) arborio or basmati rice (rinsed)
- 1 Tbsp (15 g) ghee
- ½ Tbsp cardamom (3 g)
- 1 tsp ground nutmeg (1 g)
- 1-2 Tbsp (7 – 14 g) of Pitta Spice Mix

STEP 2

- ⅛ cup (22 g) coconut sugar – or to taste – optional
- ½ cup (115 g) dates or raisins – optional

PREPARATION

1. Preheat the oven to 338º F (170º C)
2. Add all the spices to a cup with about ¼ cup (30 to 60 g) of your selected milk and mix them thoroughly so that the spices are blended in with the milk, which ensures the spices mix well in the pudding.

3. Combine the milk, the rice, the spices, and coconut sugar (if required) in a deep pot and place on a high heat, stirring from time to time until the milk is almost boiling, then pour the mixture into a deep baking dish. This method reduces the oven cooking time by about 30 minutes.
4. If not using coconut sugar then dates or raisins are required. For dates, chop them into quarters. Then add either fruit to the pan with 1 ½ cups of water (345 g) or 3 times the amount of fruit. Cook on high heat until the water is boiling. Then lower the temperature to a simmer. When the water has reduced by about a third, then take off the heat. Blend the dates or the raisins with a little water to a fine pulp and use it as a side dish so that everyone can add the sweetener to their taste.
5. Pour the rice and milk into a deep baking dish and bake it for about up to 90 minutes, stirring the pudding about every 45 minutes. This prevents the surface of the rice pudding from forming a thick skin which would prevent the water from evaporating from the milk.

Depending on the oven and the rice, it may be necessary to add a little more milk towards the end to ensure the rice pudding is at the desired consistency when it is cooked. The result is a creamy rice pudding.

Vata

Rice Pudding

🕐 2 Hours 🍴 Serves 3

Rice pudding has the potential to be balancing for many people and here we offer three versions to choose from.

1. Milk with cardamom and nutmeg
2. ½ milk and ½ of half and half cream
3. Oat milk

All these three can be sweetened with either coconut sugar or blended dates or raisins. Dates and raisins are good for both Vata and Pitta types. It is easy to try both as the date or raisin pulp can be served as a side dish with the dessert so that everyone can sweeten the pudding to their taste.

With these different types of milk and sweeteners you will have to adjust the quantity to suit your taste. The dates and raisins need about half the amount of water to give them the right consistency.

Arborio rice is traditional for rice pudding, but basmati rice is also suitable.

STEP 1

- A little under 5 cups (1200 g) milk or milk & half and half or oat milk
- ½ cup (75 g) arborio or basmati rice (rinsed)
- 1 Tbsp (15 g) ghee
- ½ Tbsp cardamom (3 g)
- 1 tsp ground nutmeg (1 g)
- 1-2 Tbsp (7 – 14 g) of Vata Spice Mix

STEP 2

- ⅛ cup (22 g) coconut sugar – or to taste – optional
- ½ cup (115 g) dates or raisins – optional

PREPARATION

1. Preheat the oven to 338º F (170º C)
2. Add all the spices to a cup with about ¼ cup (30 to 60 g) of milk and mix them thoroughly so that the spices are blended in with the milk. This will ensure the spices mix well with the pudding.
3. Combine the milk, the rice, the spices, and coconut sugar (if required) in a deep pot and place on a high heat, stirring from time to time until the milk is almost boiling, then pour

the mixture into a deep baking dish. This method reduces the oven cooking time by about 30 minutes.
4. If not using coconut sugar, then dates or raisins are required. For dates, chop them into quarters. Then add either fruit to the pan with 1½ cups of water (345 g) or 3 times the amount of fruit. Cook on high heat until the water is boiling. Then lower the temperature to a simmer. When the water has reduced by about a third, then take off the heat. Blend the dates or raisins with a little water to a fine pulp and use it as a side dish so that everyone can add the sweetener to their taste.
5. Depending on the oven and the rice it may be necessary to add a little more milk towards the end for the desired consistency. The result is a very creamy rice pudding.

Kapha

Rice Pudding

🕐 2 Hours   🍴 Serves 3

Rice pudding has the potential to be balancing for three types of constitution. In this recipe, the almond milk with a little heat from ginger is ideal for Kapha types. Most people are either Kapha/Pitta or Pitta/Kapha, and this is why some sweet almond milk is often suitable for these types of people. Pure Kapha only is very rare.

STEP 1

- ¼ (30 g) almond milk
- ½ Tbsp (3 g) cardamom
- 1 tsp (1 g) ground nutmeg
- 3 Tbsp ground ginger

STEP 2

- A little under 5 cups (1200 g) almond milk
- ½ cup (75 g) arborio rice (rinsed)

PREPARATION

1. Preheat the oven to 338º F (170º C)
2. Add all the spices to about a ¼ cup of almond milk and mix them thoroughly so that the spices are blended in with the milk, which ensures the spices mix well with the pudding.
3. Combine the milk, the rice and the spices in a deep pot and place on a high heat, stirring from time to time until the milk is almost boiling, then pour the mixture into a deep baking dish.
4. Place the dish into the oven and bake it for about up to 90 minutes, stirring the pudding about every 45 minutes. This prevents the surface of the rice pudding from forming a thick skin which would prevent the water from evaporating from the milk.
5. Depending on the oven and the rice, it may be necessary to add a little more milk towards the end to ensure the rice pudding is at the desired consistency when it is cooked. This leads to a creamy rice pudding.

Vata

Pear Crumble

🕐 70 minutes   🍴 Serves 4

STEP

- 5 cups (720 g) 5–6 pears, peeled and chopped into large pieces
- ¼ cup (45 g) stewed raisins (optional)

STEP 2

- 1 cup (135 g) salted butter

STEP 3

- 1 cup (75 g) quick oats
- ½ cup (120 g) rice flour
- 1 cup (60 g) ground almonds
- ¼ cup (48 g) coconut sugar
- 1 Tbsp (7 g) Vata Spice Mix
- ½ Tbsp (6 g) ground cinnamon
- ½ tsp (2 g) ground cloves
- ½ tsp (2.5 g) salt – or to taste

PREPARATION

1. Preheat the oven to 350º F (180º C). Boil the chopped pears until the pears are just tender. Then set aside. Boil the raisins in ⅓ of a cup of water for about 10 minutes, until the water has just boiled off.
2. Steps 2 & 3 are for the topping. Melt the butter in a pan large enough to hold all the other ingredients, then take off the heat. Add all the topping ingredients in Step 3 to the pan and mix thoroughly.
3. Combine the pears with the raisins (if used) and place in a 7 x 5 baking dish lined with parchment paper or buttered. Then lay the topping over the pears without patting it down.
4. Bake for 20–25 minutes. After 20 minutes, check the topping. When it is crispy around the edges, the crumble is ready.

Pitta

Apple Crumble

🕐 45 minutes   🍴 Serves 4

STEP 1

- 5 cups (5–6 apples) (720 g) peeled and chopped into 8 pieces per apple
- ¼ cup (45 g) raisins (optional)
- Step 2
- ¾ cup (135 g) salted butter

STEP 3

- 1 cup (75 g) quick oats
- ½ cup (120 g) rice flour
- ⅔ cup (60 g) desiccated coconut
- ⅓ cup (48 g) coconut sugar
- 1 Tbsp (7 g) Pitta Spice Mix
- 2 tsp (4 g) cardamom
- ½ tsp (1 g) fresh nutmeg
- a little over ¼ tsp (1.5 g) salt – or to taste

PREPARATION

1. Preheat the oven to 350º F (180º C). Boil the chopped apples until they are just tender. Then set aside. Boil the raisins in ⅓ of a cup of water for about 10 minutes, until the water has just boiled off.
2. Steps 2 & 3 are for the topping. Melt the butter in a pan large enough to hold all the other ingredients, then take off the heat. Add all the topping ingredients in Step 3 to the pan and mix thoroughly.
3. Combine the apples with the raisins (if used) and place in an oblong baking dish about 7 x 5 inches, lined with parchment paper or buttered. Then lay the topping over the pears without pushing it down.
4. Bake for 20–25 minutes. After 20 minutes, check the topping. When it is crispy around the edges, the crumble is ready.

Pitta

Stewed Fig & Raisin

🕐 15 minutes 🍴 Serves 4

STEP 1

- 1 cup (200 g) finely chopped fig
- 1 cup (150 g) dried raisins

PREPARATION

1. Add the fruits to a pot with 3 cups of water and simmer over medium heat for 10 minutes until all the figs are softened.
2. Blend half the fruits until smooth and mix them with the remaining fruits. This is intended to be served with custard, cream, or other stewed fruits such as apples and pears, for example.

8
Cakes

Vata

Date & Walnut Cake

🕐 80 minutes   🍴 Serves 6

STEP 1

- 1¾ cups (142 g) crushed walnuts

STEP 2

- 20 (285 g) Medjool dates
- 2 Tbsp (20 g) of the flour from step 3

STEP 3

- 3 eggs
- ½ cup & 1 tbsp (135 g) salted butter
- 1¼ tsp (5 g) salt – or to taste
- 1 cup (120 g) rice or spelt flour
- ½ cup (120 g) coconut sugar
- 1 Tbsp (10 g) baking powder
- 2 Tbsp (15 g) powdered ginger
- 1⅓ Tbsp (10 g) Vata Spice Mix
- 1⅓ Tbsp (10 g) ground cinnamon – optional

PREPARATION

1. Preheat the oven to 350º F (180º C).
2. To crush the walnuts, you can place them in a sturdy plastic bag and roll over them with a rolling pin. Then place them in a pan and add boiling water. Leave them to soak for 20 minutes. Then put them on a tray in the oven at 220º F for 10 minutes to dry. It is important that the walnuts are cooled down, at room temperature, before adding them to the cake mix, as warmth would activate the raising agent. Preparing the walnuts in this way removes the Vata-aggravating properties of dried walnuts.
3. Pit the dates and cut them into 4 pieces. Place them in a bowl and sprinkle with 2 tbsp (15 g) of flour. This gives the dates a drier surface and prevents them from sinking to the bottom of the cake as it bakes.
4. Melt the butter in a pan on very low heat and set aside. Add all the Step 3 ingredients to a large bowl and mix thoroughly, either with a spoon or with a mixer on low speed. Then with a spoon gently stir in the dates and walnuts.
5. Scoop the batter into a 9 x 5-inch cake pan, lined with parchment paper, or buttered and for 60–75 minutes. At 60 minutes, poke the center of the cake with a skewer to test

whether it is ready. When the skewer comes out clean, remove the cake from the oven and set on a rack to cool.

Vata/Pitta

Fig Cake

🕐 80 minutes 🍴 Serves 6

STEP 1

- 2 cups (225 g) dried figs

STEP 2

- 3 eggs
- ½ cup & 1 Tbsp (135 g) salted butter
- 1 Tbsp (4 g) salt, or salt – or to taste
- 1 cup (120 g) rice or spelt flour
- ½ cup (120 g) coconut sugar
- 1 Tbsp (10 g) baking powder

For Vata:

- 1⅓ cup (10 g) ground cinnamon

For Pitta:

- 1⅓ cup (10 g) ground fennel

PREPARATION

1. Preheat the oven to 350º F (175ºC).
2. Remove the fig heads and discard. Then chop the figs into quarters. Ideally, soak them overnight, or boil them in a little water until tender. Then set aside to cool. Next, mix the figs with 2 tbsp (20 g) of flour.
3. Melt the butter in a pan over very low heat and set aside. Place all the Step 2 ingredients—except the eggs, the raising agent, and butter—in a large bowl and mix thoroughly. Then add the melted butter, the raising agent, and the eggs and mix thoroughly either by hand or with an electric mixer on low speed.
4. Scoop the batter into a 9 x 5-inch cake pan, lined with parchment paper or buttered. Combine the dates with the cake mix and place the mixture in the cake pan. Bake for 50–70 minutes. After 50 minutes, poke the center of the cake with a skewer. When it comes out clean, the cake is done.

Vata/Pitta

Cherry & Almond Cake

🕐 80 minutes   🍴 Serves 6

STEP 1

- 4 cups (225 g) whole unsweetened cherries
- ½ cup & 1 Tbsp (135 g) salted butter

STEP 2

- 3 eggs
- 1⅔ cups (175g) ground almonds
- 1 tsp (4 g) salt – or to taste
- 1 cup (120 g) rice or spelt flour
- ½ cup (120 g) coconut sugar
- 1 Tbsp (10 g) baking powder

Vata:

- 2 Tbsp (15 g) Vata Spice Mix

Pitta:

- 2 Tbsp (15 g) Pitta Spice Mix

PREPARATION

1. Melt the butter in a pan on very low heat and set aside. Cut the cherries in halves and mix them in a bowl with 2 ½ tbsp (20 g) of flour.
2. Set the oven to 350º F (175º C).
3. In a large bowl, mix together all the ingredients listed in Step 2 except the eggs and the baking powder. Then, add the eggs, the baking powder and melted butter. Mix thoroughly, using a spoon or an electric mixer on low speed. Finally, fold in the cherries carefully.
4. Pour the batter into a 9 x 5-inch cake pan lined with parchment paper or buttered. Bake for 55–65 minutes. After 50 minutes, poke the cake with a skewer to test whether it is ready. When the skewer comes out clean, remove the cake from the oven and set on a rack to cool.

Pitta

Coconut Cake

🕐 80 minutes 🍴 Serves 6

STEP 1

- ⅞ cup (200 g) creamed coconut (1 packet)
- ⅔ cup (150 g) salted butter

STEP 2

- 3 eggs
- 2 cups (170 g) desiccated coconut
- 1 tsp (4.25 g) salt – or to taste
- 1 cup (120 g) rice or spelt flour
- ½ cup (120 g) coconut sugar
- 1 Tbsp (10 g) baking powder
- 1⅓ Tbsp (10 g) Pitta Spice Mix

PREPARATION

1. Preheat the oven to 350°F (180°C).
2. Melt the butter in a pan over low heat and set aside. Some creamed coconut packets come in solid form and at room temperature, while others come in liquid form, sometimes chilled. If yours is solid, chop it into small pieces and place in a pan over low heat, stirring constantly to enable the creamed coconut to melt. Then remove from heat.
3. Add all the ingredients listed in Steps 1 and 2 to a bowl and mix thoroughly, either by hand or with an electric mixer on low speed.
4. Scoop the batter into a 9 x 5-inch cake pan, lined with parchment paper or buttered. Bake for 55–65 minutes. At about 50 minutes, poke the center of the cake with a skewer to test whether it is ready. When the skewer comes out clean, remove the cake from the oven and set on a rack to cool.

Pitta

Date Cake

🕐 80 minutes   🍴 Serves 6

STEP 1

- 24 (320 g) Medjool dates
- ½ cup & 1 Tbsp (135 g) salted butter

STEP 2

- 3 eggs
- 1 tsp (4.25 g) salt – or to taste
- 1 cup (120 g) rice or spelt flour
- ⅔ cup (120 g) coconut sugar
- 1 Tbsp (10 g) baking powder
- 2 Tbsp (15 g) Pitta Spice Mix

PREPARATION

1. Preheat the oven to 350º F (175ºC).
2. Pit the dates and cut them into 4–6 pieces. Then add all the dates to a bowl and mix thoroughly with about 2 tbsp (20 g) of rice flour. This will help to keep the dates from sinking to the bottom of the cake. Melt the butter in a pan on very low heat and set aside.
3. Place the ingredients in Step 2 in a mixing bowl—except the eggs and baking powder. Mix thoroughly. Then, add the eggs and baking powder and continue mixing, either by hand or in a food processor on low speed.
4. Pour the batter into a 9 x 5-inch cake pan lined with parchment paper, or buttered. Bake for 55–75 minutes. After about 50 minutes, poke the middle of the cake with a skewer to test whether it is fully baked. When the skewer comes out clean, remove the cake from the oven and set on a rack to cool.

Kapha

Spicy Apricot Cake

🕐 80 minutes   🍴 Serves 6

STEP 1

- 1 ⅔ cups (250 g) dried apricots

STEP 2

- 3 large eggs
- ½ cup (80 g) sunflower oil
- 1 tsp (4 g) salt – or to taste
- ½ cup (120 g) butter
- 1 cup (120 g) rice or spelt flour
- 1 Tbsp (10 g) baking powder
- 3 Tbsp (20g) Kapha Spice Mix

PREPARATION

1. Preheat the oven to 350º F (180 ºC).
2. Cut the apricots into 4–6 pieces. Then place ⅔ of the chopped apricots in a pan, cover with water, and soak overnight or simmer them for 5–10 minutes, until soft and moist.
3. Melt the butter in a pan over very low heat and set aside. In a large bowl, thoroughly mix all the Step 2 ingredients with the dried and soaked apricots.
4. Scoop the batter into a 9 x 5-inch cake pan, lined with parchment paper or buttered. Then pour the mixture evenly into the tin and bake for 45–60 minutes. At about 45 minutes, poke the center of the cake with a skewer to test whether it is ready. When the skewer comes out clean, remove the cake from the oven and set on a rack to cool.

9

Chutneys

Vata

Mango Chutney

🕐 15 minutes   🍴 Serves 4

STEP 1

- 2 ripe mangoes, cubed

STEP 2

- 1 Tbsp (7 g) Vata Spice Mix
- ½ Tbsp (5 g) fresh ground ginger – or to taste
- 1 tsp (4 g) mustard seed powder
- ½ Tbsp (2.5 g) cumin seeds
- 1½ Tbsp (15 g) coconut sugar
- ½ Tbsp (7 g) ghee
- ½ tsp (2 g) salt – or to taste
- 1 Tbsp (15 g) lemon juice – or to taste

PREPARATION

1. Blend thoroughly ⅔ of the mangoes. Put the blended mixture in a bowl, add the remaining mango cubes and stir.
2. Heat the ghee in a skillet. Add the cumin seeds and mustard and sauté over low heat until the seeds crackle. Remove from the heat and add all the remaining ingredients to the skillet and mix thoroughly. Then add to the bowl of mangoes and stir. The fresh chutney is ready to serve.

Pitta

Avocado & Walnut Chutney

🕐 10 minutes　🍴 Serves 3

STEP 1

- 1 (120 g) avocado, mashed
- 1½ cups (120 g) walnuts, soaked overnight and dried

STEP 2

- 1 Tbsp (7 g) Pitta Spice Mix
- ½ Tbsp (2.5g) cumin seeds
- 2 Tbsp (30 g) coconut milk
- ⅓ tsp (1.5g) salt – or to taste
- 1 Tbsp (15 g) ghee
- 1 tsp (5 g) lime juice – or to taste

PREPARATION

1. In a blender, grind the walnuts into a powder.
2. Melt the ghee in a pan, add the spices and stir until the spices have heated up. Then, add all the other ingredients of step 2 and stir continuously for about a minute. Take off the heat.
3. Add the mashed avocado and walnut powder to the pan and mix thoroughly. Serve up in a bowl with a serving spoon on the dining table.

Kapha

Apple & Apricot Chutney

🕐 15 minutes   🍴 Serves 4

STEP 1

- 4 cups (400 g) peeled and chopped apples
- ½ cup (100 g) soak the dried apricots in hot water

STEP 2

- 1 tsp (4 g) mustard seed powder – or to taste
- 1 tsp (2.5 g) Hot Kapha Spice Mix – or to taste
- 1 Tbsp (8 g) Hot Kapha Seed Mix
- 1 Tbsp (15 g) sunflower oil
- 1 tsp (4 g) powdered ginger
- ⅔ cup (3 g) salt – or to taste
- 3 tsp (15 g) lime juice – or to taste

PREPARATION

1. Add the apples to a pot with 2 cups of water and boil on a medium heat until soft and leave 1ncup of water with the fruit. Take off the heat and blend to a pulp.
2. Fry the Hot Kapha Seed and Spice Mix, the ginger and the mustard seed powder in sunflower oil on a medium heat stirring continuously for about 3-4 minutes to release the flavor into the oil.
3. Chop the apricots into 6 to 8 pieces, add to the apples and blend.
4. Mix all the other ingredients in Step 2 with the fried ingredients and the fruit thoroughly and add it to a serving bowl. The chutney is now ready to serve.

10

Beverages

Drinks, like food, affect our state of balance, how we feel and think and how the body functions, especially in the morning. Fluids keep the physiology hydrated, replacing valuable moisture that may be lost to evaporation, especially in dry climates. Drinking fluids also supports the digestive process, and successful digestion is the foundation of robust health. Ayurveda recommends sipping small amounts of water or other drinks with meals and also first thing in the morning. The body loses a lot of water overnight while you sleep, so as soon as you wake up, drink at least two cups of warm water to refresh the system, ease elimination, and prepare for the day.

Here are a few nice breakfast options that are especially balancing for the different dosha types.

Vata—orange juice, almond milk, oat milk
Pitta—coconut water, oat milk
Kapha—orange juice

You can also spice your beverages to enhance balance, according to these options throughout the day.

Vata—ginger, cinnamon, and/or turmeric
Pitta—licorice, turmeric, and/or cardamom
Kapha—ginger, turmeric, and/or green tea

When preparing a tea, look for these spices in the ingredients list to get the balancing effect you need.

Six Complete Meals

A FEW SAMPLE MENUS

These recipes have been created to inspire your family and friends with great tasting dishes that satisfy everyone and leave them wanting to know more about Ayurveda. If you have the suitable spice mixes available on the table, this would give each person the option of adding more to their dish if they wanted to.

Be sure to click on the recipes below well in advance so you can budget the time you need to easily manage all the tasks and ingredients, including baking or soaking times, and assure that you have the necessary equipment ready. I have planned these menus for you, so you will not need to worry about assembling a meal that meets dosha-specific and nutritional needs. These meals provide the nine essential amino acids while also assuring that the dishes complement each other in a pleasing symphony of tastes and textures. Here are six of my favorites with links to the recipes.

VATA COMPLETE MEAL 1

Main Dish:

[Mung Bean with Vegetables](URL) (URL)

[White Basmati Rice](URL) (URL)

[Vata Mango Chutney](URL) (URL)

Dessert:

[Pear Crumble with Custard](URL) (URL)

[With Lassi](URL) (URL)

VATA COMPLETE MEAL 2

Main Dish:

[Vata Nut Roast with Quinoa and Walnuts](URL) (URL)

[Kitchari with Cilantro & Cumin Seeds](URL) (URL)

[Roast Potatoes in Ghee with Rosemary](URL) (URL)

[Vata Mango Chutney](URL) (URL)

Desert:

[Date & Walnut Cake](URL) (URL)

PITTA COMPLETE MEAL 1

Main Dish:

French Lentils & Vegetables (URL Page 101) with Sweet Potato
Quinoa with Cumin Seeds (URL)
Paneer with Avocado & Tahini (URL)
Pitta Chutney with Avocado & Walnut (URL)

Desert:

Apple Crumble (URL) with Desiccated Coconut

PITTA COMPLETE MEAL 2

Main dish:

Asparagus and Zucchini Stew (URL)
Chicken Chunks (URL) with Basil
White Basmati Rice (URL)

Desert:

Date Cake (URL)

KAPHA: COMPLETE MEALS 1

Main Dish:

Brown Lentils with Vegetables (URL) & Mustard Seeds
White Basmati Rice (URL)
Apple & Apricot Chutney (URL)

Desert:

Spicy Apricot Cake (URL)

KAPHA: COMPLETE MEALS 2

Main Dish:

Spicy Eggplant & Kale
Paneer with Asparagus and Hot Kapha Spice & Seed Mixes
White Basmati Rice (URL)
Dahl

Desert:

Kapha Rice Pudding

Appendix I

CHOOSING HEALTHY PRODUCE: WATCH OUT FOR THE DIRTY DOZEN™ AND THE CLEAN FIFTEEN™

A non-profit operational watchdog called the Environmental Working Group looks at data supplied by the US Department of Agriculture and the Food and Drug Administration, and checks pesticide residues found in produce. The list is updated annually, and you can visit it at: https://www.ewg.org/foodnews/summary.php.

Both organizations supply a list of 12 fruits and vegetables that have been exposed to high doses of pesticides and contain high residues of poisons which are known to seriously damage health. These are known as "The Dirty Dozen." Also featured is a list of fruits and vegetables which are known to be relatively low in environmental toxins. These are "The Clean Fifteen." They are listed below so you can opt for the safer "clean" or go organic if you need to buy any of the "dozen."

THE DIRTY DOZEN™

1. Strawberries
2. Kale
3. Spinach
4. Apples
5. Nectarines
6. Grapes
7. Cherries
8. Peaches
9. Pears
10. Celery
11. Tomatoes
12. Potatoes

THE CLEAN FIFTEEN™

1. Sweet corn
2. Avocados
3. Onions
4. Pineapples
5. Sweet peas
6. Papayas
7. Eggplant
8. Asparagus
9. Kiwis
10. Cabbages
11. Broccoli
12. Cantaloupes
13. Cauliflower
14. Honeydew melon
15. Mushrooms

Appendix II

MEASUREMENT CONVERSION

US Standard	US Standard oz	Metric	Fahrenheit (f)	Celsius (c)
2 tablespoons	1 fl. Oz	30 mL	250 F	120 C
¼ cup	2 fl. Oz	60	300 F	150 C
½ cup	4 fl. oz	120	325 F	165 C
1 cup	8 fl. oz	240	350 F	180 C
1½ cup	12 fl. oz	355	375 F	190 C
2 cups	16 fl. oz	475	400 F	200 C
4 cups	32 fl. oz	1 L	425 F	220 C
1 quarter	33 fl. oz		450 F	230 C
1 gallon	128 fl. oz	4 L		

US Standard	Metric Approx.	US Standard	Metric Approx.
⅛ teaspoon	0.5 ml	½ ounce	15 g
¼ teaspoon	1 ml	1 ounce	30 g
½ teaspoon	2 ml	2 ounce	60 g
¾ teaspoon	4 ml	4 ounce	115 g
1 teaspoon	5 ml	8 ounce	225 g
1 tablespoon	15 ml	12 ounces	340 g
¼ cup	59 ml	16 ounces (1 pound)	455 g
⅓ cup	79 ml		
½ cup	118 ml		
⅔ cup	156 ml		
¾ cup	177 ml		
1 cup	235 ml		
2 cups (1 pint)	475 ml		
3 cups	700 ml		
4 cups	1 L		

Printed in Great Britain
by Amazon